HUD, NORMA RAE, and THE LONG, HOT SUMMER

Three Screenplays by
Irving Ravetch
and
Harriet Frank, Jr.

Edited and with an Introduction by
Michael R. Frank

Foreword by
Martin Ritt

A PLUME BOOK

NEW AMERICAN LIBRARY

NEW YORK AND SCARBOROUGH, ONTARIO

NAL BOOKS ARE AVAILABLE AT QUANTITY DISCOUNTS WHEN USED TO PROMOTE PRODUCTS OR SERVICES. FOR INFORMATION PLEASE WRITE TO PREMIUM MARKETING DIVISION, NEW AMERICAN LIBRARY, 1633 BROADWAY, NEW YORK, NEW YORK 10019.

PLUME TRADEMARK REG. U.S. PAT. OFF. AND FOREIGN COUNTRIES
REGISTERED TRADEMARK—MARCA REGISTRADA
HECHO EN CHICAGO, U.S.A.

SIGNET, SIGNET CLASSIC, MENTOR, ONYX, PLUME, MERIDIAN and NAL BOOKS are published *in the United States* by NAL PENGUIN INC., 1633 Broadway, New York, New York 10019, *in Canada* by The New American Library of Canada Limited, 81 Mack Avenue, Scarborough, Ontario M1L 1M8

Library of Congress Cataloging-in-Publication Data

Ravetch, Irving.
  The long, hot summer; Hud; Norma Rae.

  Filmography: p.
  1. Motion picture plays—United States. 2. Film adaptations. I. Frank, Harriet. II. Frank, Michael R. (Michael Ravetch), 1959– . III. Title: Long, hot summer. IV. Title: Hud. V. Title: Norma Rae.
PS3568.A835L6   1988   791.43'75   87-34718
ISBN 0-452-26084-1

First Printing, April, 1988

1 2 3 4 5 6 7 8 9

PRINTED IN THE UNITED STATES OF AMERICA

Contents

Foreword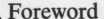

I don't know of any better screenwriters than Irving Ravetch and Harriet Frank, Jr. They are absolutely the best, on every level. I've enjoyed collaborating with them, and I know that we've done work as good as any that has been done in Hollywood. Our whole lives are intertwined in this work, from *The Long, Hot Summer*, back in the fifties, on. I am proud of the movies we've made together and consider several among them the finest of my career.

I have generally been faithful to the Ravetches' material because I respect their writing and I respect their impulses, even when at times we've disagreed. Like all good writers, Irving Ravetch and Harriet Frank, Jr., value language, but at times language has gotten in the way of what they've wanted to do in a particular scene, and I've had to ask them to make changes. Fortunately, we communicate very well. The Ravetches are sensitive to my opinion, as I am to theirs. We are strong personalities, but after all these years we speak in a kind of shorthand—we understand each other implicitly.

Irving Ravetch and Harriet Frank, Jr., believe in what they write. I also believe in what they write, and I would hire them to do any kind of picture. However, I am aware, as I think they are too, that certain things—light comedy, for example—aren't as good for them as more serious subjects. This is true of me as well. We have discovered, or perhaps developed, our strengths together.

I would never fail to do a movie with the Ravetches that they wanted to do. I might criticize, I might suggest changes, but I would make it anyway. I feel I owe them, as I feel they owe me. It's not written anywhere that we have to agree. That's not the nature of the creative process. But they are my friends and my genuine collaborators, and I believe the body of our work reflects the success of this collaboration.

—Martin Ritt

Acknowledgments

For their contributions to this project, I would like to thank Ron Nolte, Ron Mardigian, and Hal Ross at the William Morris Agency; Larrayne Jurist at 20th Century Fox and David Rosenbaum at Paramount; Larry McMurtry; Henry P. Leifermann; Random House, Inc., for the William Faulkner estate; Martin Ritt; Tamara Asseyev; and, for their continuing support, Gloria Loomis and Beth Vesel.

Introduction

It all began, for Irving Ravetch, one rainy Saturday in New York, when as a boy of nine he was taken by his Aunt Selma to a midtown picture palace where the words *Garbo Talks* were emblazoned on its marquee. These served as a beacon to the tide of people in the street, who seemed to loft the small boy and his companion into the majestic auditorium, with its raked floor and sparkling chandelier and its rug patterned with red and yellow feathers. The room soon went dark, conversation dwindled to a whisper, and *she* appeared—she whose photograph hung next to the mirror over Aunt Selma's bureau, so that their profiles could be compared. When she spoke, the aunt gasped and pinched the nephew, and with this pinch—of joy or shock or profound recognition—the memory grows dim. Next, the boy is older—twelve, thirteen, gangly and shy, his legs stretched over the empty seat in front of him at the West Coast Theater in Long Beach, California. He is watching Paul Muni in *Scarface* for the third time that day and the sixth that week. He will see only *The 39 Steps* more often, so often in fact that, in the spirit of his beloved Mr. Memory, he will be able to recite much of the dialogue ahead of the actors.

For Harriet Frank, Jr., it began at the Kelso Theater near Longview, Washington, where, nestling in the lap of her Grandpa Sol, she watched bandits gallop across an endless Mojave desert. While he dozed, she was transfixed by the nimble riders and their choreographed shoot-outs, the ethical sheriff and his foil, who always, always dressed in black. Twice a week, on Thursdays and Saturdays, this weary, gracious old man collected his grandchildren and took them to the movies. The habit stuck. Later, during her adolescence in a grim and depressed Portland, Harriet and her brother rode the streetcar downtown every weekend, past the soup lines and the grizzled men selling apples, past the cardboard shacks along the Willamette River, to lose themselves in the antics of Katharine Hepburn or the splendor of Astaire and Rogers. At the Paramount Theater on Broadway, a dime opened up a world: a live prelude by Fanchon and Marco, with singers and dancers and a magician who sawed through spangled ladies; two shorts; and the much-anticipated feature—*Wuthering Heights, Dark Victory, It Happened One Night*—new and dazzling each week.

"It," of course, is a love of the movies, a passion for those reels of flickering celluloid whose talking era is roughly contemporary with these writers themselves. Irving Ravetch and Harriet Frank, Jr., have worked as screenwriters in Hollywood for over forty years, thirty of them together as line-for-line collaborators on such movies as *The Long, Hot Summer, Hud, Hombre, The Reivers, The Cowboys, Conrack, Norma Rae*, and *Murphy's Romance*, among others. For talented and bookish English majors at UCLA in the early forties, all roads seemed to lead to the motion picture studios, to Carl Laemmle's Universal on the other side of the Hollywood Hills, to the gated Paramount down on Melrose Avenue to sprawling Metro-Goldwyn-Mayer in Culver City. It was at M-G-M that Ravetch and Frank met. Frank's mother, Harriet, Sr., was a story editor at M-G-M, where she read and digested potential movie material—stories, novels, plays—then delivered a brief, dramatic synopsis to Louis B. Mayer for his instant approval or rejection. She arranged for her daughter to join the studio's Junior Writers' Program, in which young writers were given immediate hands-on experience revising, polishing, and occasionally even completing finished scripts of their own. Irving Ravetch was a shorts writer at the time, assigned to such two-reel series as *Crime Does Not Pay*, where his task was to demonstrate the titular maxim in thirteen minutes or less.

The Ravetches were married in 1946. During the next ten years they served a varied and for the most part separate apprenticeship. Ravetch wrote and adapted Western stories while Frank worked as a hired hand at several studios; at one point, never having seen so much as a round in her life, Harriet Frank, Jr., was given the job of toughening up the dialogue in a Dane Clark fight picture. While Ravetch made an ultimately unsuccessful venture into the Broadway theater, Frank supported the couple by writing magazine fiction, which she published in *Collier's, Good House-*

keeping, and *The Saturday Evening Post*. Their screenwriting collaboration began in 1957, when Jerry Wald, the producer whose much-publicized goal was to make movies out of all the world's literary classics, optioned *The Hamlet* by William Faulkner and asked Ravetch and Frank to dramatize it. The eventual result, *The Long, Hot Summer*, was their breakthrough.

It was also the beginning of another significant collaboration, the one between the Ravetches and the director Martin Ritt. Originally an actor, later a director and a teacher, Ritt was a member of the Group Theater and one of the founders of the Actor's Studio in New York, where he and Irving Ravetch met. Ritt had directed *Edge of the City*, and it was this, together with his work in the theater, that encouraged the Ravetches to suggest him to Jerry Wald as their preferred director for *The Long, Hot Summer*. The Ravetches and Ritt have collaborated on seven movies, and it is probably fair to say that they've done their strongest work together. From the point of view of the screenwriter, and of the screenplay as a written text, Martin Ritt is perhaps the ideal director. Because of his training in the theater, Ritt has profound respect for the written word. Unlike many movie directors, he believes in rehearsal, he improvises sparingly, and he tries wherever possible to retain the dialogue as written. He is, according to Harriet Frank, Jr., "a writer's director, dedicated to preserving the intention of a screenplay, often down to the level of the individual line. As a director he is without ego, and he approaches us as writers in the same spirit." This deep, reciprocal esteem becomes particularly important during filming, when the demands of staging the written scene often necessitate its modification. Among directors Ritt is rare in his desire to have the writers on hand at all times. "If something needs fixing," he says, "I want it fixed by the best people I know." Collaboration between Ritt and the Ravetches is collaboration in its truest and most fertile sense.

Irving Ravetch and Harriet Frank, Jr., have written close to thirty scripts in their career—many more, as is the case with most screenwriters, than they have ever seen filmed. Most of their scripts, like most of their realized movies, have been adapted from outside source material, so theirs would seem to be a gift for transforming and dramatizing stories rather than generating them. And yet, when the original material is compared to the ensuing screenplay, this observation does not hold up entirely; adaptation, as practiced by the Ravetches, is often a matter of invention. If Ravetch and Frank's screenplays ultimately bear little resemblance to their sources, why begin with the sources in the first place? Ravetch explains: "We have found that, as screenwriters, we've often needed an outside story to get us started. It sparks us; it sets us in motion. In the end, we may salvage only one or two elements—a character perhaps, or a situation, or a few strong scenes—and on this we build a whole new drama." But is it not a desecration of a great book—*The Hamlet*, for example—to make such monumental changes? "Absolutely not. We can't desecrate Faulkner; no one can. *The Hamlet* will always remain intact. It is a great, potent, living work of literary fiction, there forever on the shelf. It spawned a movie, but neither, really, owes anything to the other." Harriet Frank, Jr., adds: "Faulkner was himself a screenwriter and understood the necessity of making a wide departure. The two forms are very different. You can't feel that a book is sacrosanct. The demands of drama require a whole new set of rules."

The Hamlet is a novel of 366 pages; *The Long, Hot Summer*, like most screenplays, is fewer than 120 pages in its edited version. *The Hamlet*, as a work of prose—William Faulkner's prose—is linguistically heightened, rich, and poetic, perhaps more dramatic in its depiction of psychology and emotion than in its depiction of events. *The Long, Hot Summer*, as a dramatic work, is linguistically unbuttoned, vivid, and colloquial; it can depict psychology and emotion only through events, by turning them into scenes. *The Hamlet* is a panoramic narrative in which Faulkner charts the Snopes's infiltration of Frenchman's Bend by taking up, in sequence, individual stories that sometimes do and sometimes do not overlap. Because of the much more limited time and scope at their disposal, movies tend to falter when they use a panoramic approach, so *The Long, Hot Summer* pares the original down and focuses on fewer characters. All of this is basic to the process of adaptation from book to screen. Where Ravetch and Frank differ is in their determination to find a way for the screenplay to take on an intense dramatic life of its own, even if this means reshaping or even sacrificing the intentions of the source. They believe their chief responsibility, as craftsmen, is to the movie.

The Ravetches conceived of *The Long, Hot Summer* (1958) as a romantic melodrama. Since *The Hamlet* is largely a brooding reflection on the mythic and villainous Snopes family, they chose to transform smarmy Flem Snopes into a more appealing rogue. Ben Quick retains Flem Snopes's shrewdness, but he is mischievous rather than sinister, and romantic where Snopes was merely dark. Ben Quick's name is taken from an ancillary character in *The Hamlet*, the operator of a sawmill, but he has no quality in common with this man. His shadowy antecedent is Snopes, with whom he shares a reputation for barn burning and a knack for manipulating the Varners, who own or control every enterprise in the small hamlet of Frenchman's Bend. But where Flem Snopes aims to cheat everyone in town, including members of his own large family, Ben Quick is a loner, a wanderer who only wants to trade farming for storekeeping. Although he tricks Jody Varner into buying the old Frenchman's place in the Snopes style, he ends up working with instead of against Will Varner, and he is more interested in seducing Varner's daughter Clara than in devouring the people around him.

With Ben Quick as the hero of *The Long, Hot Summer*, most of the events in *The Hamlet* no longer pertain, and the screenplay sets out to chart its own ground. Faulkner's Jody Varner, with his "air of invincible and inviolable bachelordom" becomes the sex-crazed husband to Eula, an emphatic contrast to his unmarried and, it is suggested, rather repressed sister Clara, who is an addition to the story. Will Varner, "thin as a fence rail and almost as long," becomes "a huge man, powerful by virtue of his size and his immense energy, his gargantuan appetite for life." In short, Orson Welles. Married in the novel, in the movie he has a mistress, another pairing in this screenplay which carefully opposes appetites expressed (Jody and Eula; Varner and Minnie) and appetites denied (Clara and Alan; Alan's frustrated sister Agnes). Where Quick will place between these two groups and whether he will manage to charm cool Clara Varner is the source of the movie's romantic tension, all of it supplied by the screenwriters. Indeed, the debt here to Faulkner is surprisingly modest. He is responsible for the setting, Frenchman's Bend, and Will Varner's domination of the hamlet; the scene in which Quick auctions Varner's wild horses to the gullible townspeople; and the artfully "buried" treasure at the old Frenchman's place, which dupes Jody into buying the ruined and worthless mansion from Quick for $1,000.

Martin Ritt has pointed out that an unacknowledged influence on *The Long, Hot Summer* was Tennessee Williams, or at least the Tennessee Williams of *Cat on a Hot Tin Roof*. It is true that many of the more theatrical scenes, notably the arguments between Varner and Jody, in which father and son thrash out a lifetime of resentment and antagonism, seem to recall the embittered battles between Big Daddy and Brick more than they do anything in *The Hamlet*, but the influence is perhaps less Williams's in particular than it is the American theater of the 1940s and 1950s in general. *The Long, Hot Summer* is the Ravetches' most theatrical screenplay by far: in its uncut version it runs to 150 pages; the dialogue, though naturally far simpler than Faulkner's prose, is not nearly as lean as it will become in later screenplays—*Norma Rae*, for example; and many of its more heightened moments play in or near a single setting, the Varner house, which alludes to a long line of houses in the American theater—the Tyrones', the Lomans'—where proximity often breeds confrontation. *The Long, Hot Summer* is not a movie, according to Ritt, that either he or the Ravetches would make today: "While the intention of the scenes is very strong and very specific, there is just too much language." This reflection is an interesting indication of the changes in moviemaking and moviegoing styles in the past thirty years, since it was specifically the language that was praised by contemporary reviewers. Bosley Crowther commented in *The New York Times* that "Irving Ravetch and Harriet Frank, Jr., have developed a tight, word-crackling script that lines up the bitter situation in quick scenes and slashing dialogue," and in the *New York Herald Tribune* Paul V. Beckley called the screenplay "remarkably deft" and "beautifully written." Certainly the most welcome praise of all came from Faulkner himself, who called *The Long, Hot Summer* a "charmin' little movie."

The relationship between Larry McMurtry's first novel, *Horseman, Pass By*, and the screenplay for *Hud* (1963), the movie derived from it, is in many ways a subtler one. Irving Ravetch found the material and formed a production company with Martin Ritt in order to preserve as much control as possible over the final movie, a prescient decision in view of the corrosive nature of the central character and the unsparing ending they intended to film. *Horseman, Pass By* is a novel of flawed structure, as McMurtry himself has remarked, but it did have at its core a resonant and sharply antagonistic relationship between father and son, a strong and simple setting, and a character—the heel, Hud Bannon—who had appeared in kind in a number of American movies but who had never been left unreformed at the conclusion of the drama. The plot of the novel, in which octogenarian cattle rancher Homer Bannon loses his herd to hoof-and-mouth disease while his grandson Lon comes of age watching Homer and Hud play out a long history of enmity, is essentially the same in the book and the movie. Where the screenplay departs from the novel is in the intense way it focuses the moral examples in Lon's life. *Hud* is sharply and finally about the battle for a boy's soul.

The Hud of the novel and the Hud of the movie are rough equivalents. Smooth, seductive, unprincipled, both feel no compunction about selling off the diseased cattle, for instance, even if it means infecting the entire United States. In *Horseman, Pass By*, however, having driven his mother to Temple for an operation, Hud is absent as this bleak drama unfolds. In the movie, the mother is eliminated, and Hud is lassoed back into the story so that the two points of view, Hud's moral recklessness and Homer's hard integrity, are clearly and immediately delineated. In the screenplay a back story has been added to sharpen the conflict between Granddad and Hud: Hud is given a brother, Norman, whose death he caused by driving home drunk one night fifteen years before the drama begins. The movie's Hud has a more developed flair with women; it is one of the traits his shy nephew longs to emulate. Halmea, the black housekeeper in *Horseman, Pass By*, becomes the white Alma of *Hud*; desired by both uncle and nephew, she has a sly, bantering rapport with Hud that is absent in the novel, where Hud is more superficially lecherous and succeeds in raping her. On the screen he is thwarted in this, though we recognize that a violation has taken place nonetheless. Also treated more obliquely in the movie is Granddad's death. In the novel McMurtry implies that Hud shoots Homer, ostensibly to end his misery after he breaks his leg. Lon finds an ejected shell lying in the road and tells us directly in the epilogue that "they were going to try to indict him for murder without malice." In the screenplay this scene is less obvious: Hud does not *need* to shoot his father. "He couldn't've made it any way in the world. He couldn't've made it another hour," Hud tells Lon, who responds, "He could if he'd wanted to. You fixed it so he didn't want to anymore." The destruction of the father by the son is figurative and more chilling as a result.

For Martin Ritt *Hud* is the most successful movie he and the

Ravetches have made together because there isn't a romantic moment in the script. He believes that the absence of the romantic allows the movie a chance to go deeper: "I have a chance, the actors have a chance, the visuals have a chance. There is no excess to interfere with the seriousness of the drama." Indeed, *Hud*, with its scant six minutes of score, is probably Ritt's most visual movie. Photographed in black and white by James Wong Howe, who won an Oscar for his work, the movie has a flat, empty look that suits the spareness of the dry Texas landscape as well as the severity of the story—every moment is made to count. "I knew *Hud* was first class as we went," Ritt says. "I was convinced, as we all were, of the fundamentally truthful evaluation of the central character. This was the script's strongest quality. Its impulse was the Ravetches'. They had grown up seeing movies where Clark Gable played Hud for about half the movie and then God or Spencer Tracy or some girl came along and converted him. They took *Hud* to its logical end; they refused to compromise." At its first previews *Hud* was not well received. Audiences initially resisted the movie, and Paramount asked Ritt to change the ending. "I told them I had no idea how to, but if they did, I would. Of course, I had no intention of softening the piece. Fortunately, after it was screened in New York and the reports were marvelous, the studio decided to leave it alone."

Although they ultimately lauded *Hud*, many contemporary critics began by forewarning their readers that this was a movie in which the central character would not be redeemed. It is a measure of the way movies tend to condition responses in their audiences that they felt obliged to do so, but it is also a credit to their judgment that these critics almost universally recognized *Hud* as an advance: an unspoken rule of Hollywood, which held that stars would only play attractive figures, appeared to have been shattered. Calling it "the year's most powerful film," the *Times*'s Bosley Crowther qualified his comment by adding that this was "a daring endorsement for a picture in which the principal character is a heel." He then felt free to say that *Hud* was "as wide and profound a contemplation of the human condition as one of the New England plays of Eugene O'Neill." Other reviewers were concerned that the screenplay did not supply all the necessary motivations, that it did not explain why Hud and his father felt such hatred for each other. Yet evading exposition was another stylistic advance, one we have since come to take for granted in movies. James Powers, writing in *The Holly-*

wood Reporter, seemed troubled by the movie's "legitimate and deliberate air of mystery" but went on to remark that "the few important people involved are so vivid in the present that their past is not so vital as it otherwise would be." The writing, which brought the Ravetches their first Oscar nomination and for which they were given the New York Film Critics' Award, was singled out everywhere for specific praise. Powers said that the dialogue was "cutting sharp, colloquial, earthy," with sentences "flung like they were meant to sting." An anonymous reviewer in the London *Times* called the script "sharp and witty," and Penelope Gilliatt, writing in the London *Observer*, said that the screenplay represented "American writing at its abrasive best." For her, as for many critics, *Hud* was "the most sober and powerful film from America in a long time."

Of the three movies under consideration here, *Norma Rae* (1979) in many ways best illustrates Ravetch and Frank's strengths as screenwriters. Factual material can be a great hindrance to the screenwriter who feels, justifiably, that he owes more allegiance to a true story than to an invented one, and yet concerns about fidelity and the degree to which the truth can be manipulated often end up diminishing the drama rather than enhancing it. Two producers, Tamara Asseyev and Alex Rose, brought the Ravetches journalist Henry P. Leifermann's book about Crystal Lee Jordan, the North Carolina mill worker on whose life *Norma Rae* was based. The facts of Crystal Lee's life parallel almost exactly the facts of Norma Rae's: she was born to two generations of Southern textile mill workers and had a father whose interest in her romantic life verged on the menacing. She was married and widowed young, she had a number of children by different men, and she married a second time for convenience rather than for love. A fiesty woman, she was always vocal about the things that displeased her at work, but it wasn't until organizer Eli Zivkovich came to town to try to unionize the J.P. Stevens mill that her defiance began to have an effect. From Crystal Lee's experiences came the most stirring moments in *Norma Rae*: the scene in which Norma copies a letter the mill's bossmen have written in an attempt to stimulate conflict between black and white workers; the scene in which she stands up with her "UNION" sign, is arrested, and taken to jail; and the scene in which she tells her children about her reckless past.

Norma Rae owes a good deal to these brave moments in Crystal Lee's life, but these moments alone do not—could not—animate the movie. Its emotional resonance is the contribution of the screenwriters, who chose, as always, to concentrate on the relationships between the characters. Stubborn, independent, and funny, Norma Rae clearly needed a match, and this she was given in Reuben Warshovsky, the union organizer from New York. Warshovsky is a type, an urban Jew, a reader of books, a man of clear principles. Placed in the Southern landscape and, more importantly, opposite Norma Rae Webster, he becomes fresh—we discover him along with Norma Rae, almost as if we had never met him or his kind before. Theirs is an equal exchange; by the end of the movie each has broadened the other. It is also characteristic of a device we find in *The Long, Hot Summer* and *Hud* as well: the use of an unconsummated romantic relationship. The Ravetches treat these pairings differently in each movie. Ben Quick and Clara Varner spar, Hud and Alma are openly hostile, and the attraction between Norma and Reuben is painstakingly unacknowledged. But the approach shares a recurring interest in keeping man and woman apart. "The pursuit is invariably more intriguing than the capture," says Harriet Frank, Jr. "At least from a dramatic point of view. And the romantic relationship that is never defined as such may be the most intriguing of all."

Stories with causes are not often popular in Hollywood, and *Norma Rae* was turned down by five stars before Ritt and the Ravetches decided to take a chance on a former television actress, Sally Field. "When you cast an actor, you key into the big scenes, and if they're there, the rest of it is going to work," Ritt explains. "We cast Sally because she was a kind of a mutt, a tough woman, committed to her own kids. And, like Norma Rae, she wanted desperately to be first class. All the aspirations in Sally's personal life related to the aspirations that were implicit in making this movie work." Which, by most accounts, it did. Sally Field won her first Oscar for *Norma Rae*. The picture and the screenplay were nominated for the award, and the movie received one review in particular that recognized the significance of the Ravetches' contribution. Writing in *The New Republic*, Stanley Kauffman said that *Norma Rae* was "an exceptionally good picture, heartening in several ways, shining with several talents, but its values begin with its script. . . .

And that script provides a pleasure rare in films: it moves us about matters that concern us intellectually."

As he reviewed the list of Irving Ravetch and Harriet Frank, Jr.'s, screenplays, Kauffmann remarked that their scripts have usually shown "atmospheric intelligence, an ear for kinetic dialogue, and a motion toward important troubles," and he identified two recurring concerns in their work: social themes and the South. How did two urban Californians develop such a strong interest in Southern culture and narrative? Irving Ravetch says, "I don't really know how it came about. As I look back on my experience of the motion picture business, it seems a total accident, a wholly circumstantial affair. Apparently, we are attracted to certain kinds of American material, Southern stories but Southwestern and Western ones as well. Perhaps it's something as basic as the landscape." Harriet Frank, Jr. adds, "Marty Ritt says that in rural America the simple verities seem unusually strong. Political, social, and emotional history seems to have been made more vividly in rural settings than in urban ones." Irving Ravetch again: "One possible explanation is that we admire William Faulkner above all other American writers, and early on we adapted three of his novels [in addition to *The Hamlet*, they were *The Sound and the Fury* (1959) and *The Reivers* (1970)]. It may be that Faulkner got us stuck in the South, forever trying to capture his spirit or one close to his. We owe him a tremendous debt."

When he accepted the Irving Thalberg Award during the 1987 Oscars ceremony, Steven Spielberg, the filmmaker who has possibly taken movies farthest away from their literary and theatrical origins, announced that the time had come for these origins to be retrieved. "I think we've partially lost something we now have to reclaim," he said. "Movies have been the literature of my life, but the literature of Thalberg's generation was books and plays. They read the great words of great men." The Spielberg manifesto does not yet seem to have produced many palpable results (as if a speech could ever affect studio policy), but Hollywood is fortunate to have had in its midst writers who never lost sight of one of the more provocative and interesting sources for American movies, its rich indigenous literature. Irving Ravetch and Harriet Frank, Jr., rank favorably among these writers. In a medium where language is not held in particularly high esteem, they have persevered in crafting screenplays of quality and integrity, understanding, with most seasoned filmmakers, that no first-rate movie has ever been made without a first-rate script. Writing of excellence is not something Hollywood is known for, but it has been produced, as I think these screenplays demonstrate.

—Michael R. Frank

Editor's Note:

In editing these screenplays, I have followed the finished movies with respect to scene order and content. Scenes that were trimmed or shuffled around are trimmed or shuffled around here; scenes that were cut from the shooting script do not appear.

I have left the dialogue intact as far as possible except where, for reasons of logic or length, the movie differs vastly from the script. Although actors may not always speak a line precisely as it is written, I saw no reason to let their departures affect the printed text.

—MRF

The Long,
Hot Summer

Produced by Jerry Wald, *The Long, Hot Summer* was released by Twentieth Century Fox in 1958. Its cast included:

Ben Quick..................................... Paul Newman
Clara Varner .... Joanne Woodward
Jody Varner............................... Anthony Franciosa
Varner .... Orson Welles
Eula Varner................................... Lee Remick
Minnie .... Angela Lansbury
Alan Stewart............................. Richard Anderson
Agnes Stewart .... Sarah Marshall
Mrs. Stewart .... Mabel Albertson
Ratliff....................................... J. Pat O'Malley
Lucius .... William Walker

FADE IN:

BEFORE THE MAIN TITLES

EXT. BARN—DUSK
An old barn. It is gaunt, weathered, lofted, and it stands in clear outline against a sky in which a full moon shines. An angular post fence stretched at a crazy tilt to the horizon. No sound, no wind, no breath of movement—only a brooding old barn, long dried out.

And now, quickly, an ominous change. Through the cracks in its split boards a light begins to glow from within. It grows brighter. Suddenly, with a VOOM, like an explosion, the barn begins to flame. There is flame, crackle and smoke, fire roaring up and out against the stars and the far dark spaces of the night. Black smoke drifts over a silver moon.

INT.—CLOSE SHOT—HARRIS—MORNING
His accusing finger is thrust out; his voice is shaking with rage.

HARRIS

It was him! *He* did it!

INT. PORCH—SMALL COUNTRY STORE AT CROSSROADS—
MORNING
Harris' finger stabs at Ben Quick, leaning against the door with an affable smile on his face.

A throng of men stand as angry witnesses. There is a feeling of lynch in the air as they look with hatred at young Quick. White-bearded, in shirt and suspenders, clutching a gavel, the elderly JUSTICE OF THE PEACE holds court seated on a nail keg.

> HARRIS
> *(apoplectic)*
> . . . Then his hog got in my corn again. He had no fence that would hold it. So I put the hog in my pen. I told him he could have the hog back when he paid me a dollar pound fee . . .

> JUSTICE
> What did he say to that?

> HARRIS
> He didn't say nothin'! But last night I got his answer, all right. My barn burned!

All eyes are on Ben Quick. The elderly justice looks at him with contempt.

> JUSTICE
> A barn burner is the meanest, lowest creature there is.
> *(pauses)*
> I can't find against you, Quick. There's no proof. But I can give you advice. Leave this county and don't come back to it.

> BEN
> *(grinning)*
> You're the judge.

> JUSTICE
> That'll do! Take your belongin's and get out before dark. Case dismissed.

Ben nods agreeably, walks past the grim-faced men.

UNDER MAIN TITLES

EXT. RIVER—DAY
Ben catches a ride on a freight barge going downstream, throwing his suitcases on, leaping aboard from the bank.

EXT. RIVER—DAY
Ben, on the barge, in the middle of the wide Mississippi. Tugs pull their load in the opposite direction; the brown water is a commercial highway.

EXT. RIVER—DAY
From the barge, Ben watches the shoreline pass—now green with stands of cotton and corn, now revealing the roofs and the spires of a town, the piled canvas bags of a levee.

EXT. RIVER—DAY
The barge swings into land; Ben jumps to the bank, waves his thanks, starts up an unpaved country road away from the river.

EXT. COUNTRY ROAD—DAY
As the TITLES come to an end, Ben pauses by a shade tree, puts down his luggage, lights a cigarette, squints down the open road. He waits for a lift.

The roar of a high-powered motor can be heard before the car can be seen. He waves his thumb. The huge, open vehicle goes by in a flash. Ben shrugs.

INT. CAR—MOVING SHOT—DAY
EULA, grinning impudently, slides over from the passenger's side and hits the brake with her left foot; CLARA, driving, looks at her resigned as the car slows down.

EXT. COUNTRY ROAD—DAY
The squeal of brakes up ahead has Ben running for his ride, the suitcases flapping against his legs.

MED. SHOT—THE CAR—DAY
The two girls look out at him with interest as he approaches. CLARA VARNER is twenty-three, a pretty, delicate, intelligent face; her sister-in-law, EULA VARNER, is a soft, ample girl with eyes like cloudy hot-house grapes and a full damp mouth.

> EULA
> *(friendly)*
> Like a lift to town?

> BEN
> Never walk when I can ride.

Eula indicates the back and he gets in. Clara guns the motor; they lurch away swiftly.

MOVING SHOT—INT. THE CAR—DAY
They get away so fast that Ben is thrown off balance; a great pile of bundles and packages cascade into his lap. Eula smiles at him from the front seat.

> EULA
> Just push 'em out of your way.

Ben starts piling them up neatly again.

EULA

I started shoppin' in those Memphis stores this mornin' and just went wild. Summer shoes, figured print, alligator bag—which is all a laugh, considerin' we live in Frenchman's Bend and nobody's goin' to see 'em but redneck farmers and immediate family. I don't care, though—I got my morale to keep up.

BEN
(smiling)

You two country girls?

EULA

Country? Our little town is the most *no*-where place in the whole state of Mississippi. You can believe me when I tell you it laces you in as tight as a corset. As far as social amusements are concerned, there are *none*.

BEN

Sounds fine. I'm a quiet-living man myself.

EULA

I only know one reason for livin' quiet—
(laughs)
—*that's* if you're too old to live any other way.

BEN

You two girls just take your fun where you can find it?

CLARA

Don't jump to any conclusions, young man. We're giving you a ride, and that's all we're giving you.

EULA
(cheerfully)

Where you headed?

BEN

Why, ma'am, I'll go as far as you go.

EULA

Boy, you sound as free as a bird. Doesn't he sound free as a bird, Clara?

Clara smiles slightly and is silent. But her eyes meet Ben's in the mirror.

BEN

Clara's wondering what *kind* of a bird. Aren't you, Clara?

EULA

Well, if you aren't a mind reader! Clara here is a school-teacher and mighty finicky about her reputation. She didn't want to pick you up. I said why not? There's two of us and one of him. And *she* said: he looks mean and dirty.

BEN

I'd say the lady is a real judge of character.

Clara, disconcerted, presses on the gas. The car leaps forward to eighty, eighty-five, ninety. Eula giggles.

EULA

Clara, you got no regard for the safety of your person, the way you drive this old Cadillac car. Honey, I'm gettin' a fallen kidney, joltin' around this countryside with you.

Clara says nothing, her eyes are on the road ahead.

FULL SHOT—THE CAR—DAY
alone on the highway, racing at top speed.

MOVING SHOT—FRENCHMAN'S BEND—DAY
A cotton gin reading "Varner's" is on the outskirts. They pass a two-story frame school, a lovely old church in a graceful setting. Then a hardware store with the legend "Varner's" again. They arrive in the main square. The courthouse with its statue of the Confederate soldier dominates the place. The gas station and the general store also read "Varner's."

Frenchman's Bend is a white-painted, sunny, open little village at a crossroads.

FULL SHOT—COURTHOUSE—DAY
Seated on a bench, hunkered on their heels beside a Coke machine, the locals in their faded jeans watch impassively as the Cadillac pulls to a halt in the square.

MED. SHOT—THE CAR—DAY
as Ben climbs out with his possessions, looking around curiously. His glance goes to the huge, black letters over the store—"Varner's." He looks toward the gas station—"Varner's."

He shakes his head admiringly and turns back to the two girls.

                    BEN
Looks like Varner is the man to see around here.

                    EULA
                  (grinning)
You can find him over at our house most any time.

                    BEN
                 (surprised)
You two girls belong to Varner?

                    EULA
              (a snort of laughter)
We two girls most particularly belong to Varner!

The car races away as Clara puts an end to the exchange; Eula waves good-bye with a smile and Ben is left standing alone in the square, his bags in his hands.

After a moment he starts for the courthouse.

MED. SHOT—COURTHOUSE—DAY
No one speaks as he comes among the locals. They watch him with frank interest: RATLIFF, HOUSTIN, WILK, ARMISTEAD, PEABODY. The men are of a breed—anecdotal, dry, humorous, intelligent.

                    BEN
How does a man make a living around here?

                    RATLIFF
                 (pleasantly)
Honest or dishonest?

                    BEN
Well, let me hear what's open.

                    RATLIFF
A fellow that's hard-workin' an' clean livin' can plant cotton
in the bottom land and corn along the edge of the hills. One
that ain't so particular can make whiskey in a homemade
still, and sell what he don't drink.

                    BEN
What happens if a Federal man comes by this way?

Ratliff looks at his cronies; their faces are blank.

RATLIFF

They been known to come by. They also been known to disappear.

WILK
(briefly)

Not entirely.

RATLIFF

No, not entirely. The missin' man's shoes might show up, or his hat, or maybe even his suspenders. 'Course, somebody else is wearin' 'em.
(squinting at Ben)
You a Federal man?

BEN
(laughing)

Let's say I'm a farmer, dad.

RATLIFF
(nodding)

All right, let's say so.
(pointing with a stick)
If you was to follow those tracks over there, you'd come to a tenant farm you could work, if you've a mind to. Belongs to a fellow named Varner . . .

BEN
(dryly)

What doesn't?

He picks up his suitcases and starts away. Ratliff calls after him.

RATLIFF

What's the name, boy?

BEN

Quick. Ben Quick.

Ben is gone. Ratliff stares at his feet and speaks thoughtfully to himself.

RATLIFF

Quick. Sho now. So that's him . . .

FULL SHOT—VARNER HOUSE—DAY
The Cadillac turns into the drive from the river road and crunches up the gravel toward the huge, white frame house.

EXT. HOUSE—DAY
AGNES STEWART is in the background, out on the lawn in a garden chair; she waves to the two girls getting out of the car.
Eula strikes her forehead in elaborate dismay.

> EULA
> Oh, heavenly days! Agnes Stewart called up this mornin', all nervous and fluttery, to say she was comin' over to see you this afternoon—and I forgot to tell you about it.

Clara goes across the lawn to greet her friend.

Eula strikes the HORN of the car and calls aloud to the house:

> EULA
> Jody! I'm home! And I spent all your money!

Staggering under an armful of packages, she goes into the house.

INT. VARNER HOUSE—DAY
JODY VARNER meets Eula on the stairs as she goes up; he comes immediately to help her with the bundles.

> JODY
> Hello there, honey bee. Looks like you sure had a busy day.

> EULA
> You just wait till you see what I have for you. I got you a red and white pure silk tie, one pound of brown sugar pralines, and some maroon felt bedroom slippers . . .

> JODY
> It ain't my birthday or anythin'.

He kisses the nape of her neck.

> EULA
> I just wanted you to know you were in my thoughts, down there in Memphis . . .

They go into their bedroom; the door closes behind them.

INT. BEDROOM—JODY AND EULA—DAY
as they enter. Eula sends her bundles cascading on to the bed.

EULA
Now you sit down and close your eyes and I'm goin' to model my purchases.

JODY
(suddenly intense)
You know somethin'? I hate this house when you're not in it.

EULA
Well, I'm in it now—
(triumphantly)
—and I *am* gorgeous.

With the words, she claps a white straw hat on her head and looks impudently to see if Jody likes it. He does. He sits in a chair before her, watching her with loving and admiring eyes.

A fan blows in the muggy day; the hi-fi set plays softly. Eula gets quickly out of her dress. In a black slip, she rips open another package, pulls out a dress, holds in front of her.

EULA
. . . They showed this very same one in the June *Vogue* magazine, only without all these little tucks in the back. Salesgirl said to me, "Mrs. Varner, that dress was made in heaven for you." On account of I'm so long-waisted. She said five customers had that dress on and I was the only one did anything for it. Like it?

JODY
What I like is you, honey.

He reaches for her. She slaps his hand away.

EULA
There's *more.*

JODY
There sure is, and all of it mighty pretty!

They engage in a childish romp. She laughs and twists away. He chases her.

EXT. LAWN—VARNER HOUSE—DAY
*Clara and her friend Agnes Stewart sit before the big house in the late
afternoon heat. They beat the languid air with palmetto fans; a pitcher of
lemonade warms beside them; their thin voile dresses cling to them.*

*There is music from above. They hear the sound of running feet, Eula
giggling, then Eula's voice:*

EULA'S VOICE
Oh, *Jody!*

Then silence.

AGNES
(nervously)
What in the world is goin' on up there?

CLARA
(smiling)
We don't go in much for stately quiet around here.

A shriek from above. Eula's voice is loud.

EULA'S VOICE
Where do you get so much *energy* on a day like this!

No answer. Silence again.

CLARA
That party's been going on ever since Papa left for the
hospital.

AGNES
I don't see how you can stand all that hootin' and hollerin'
and carryin' on. It would just turn me into a nervous wreck.

CLARA
Oh, well. They're young, they're in love.

AGNES
They're young? For your information, we're still on the
green side of twenty-five ourselves.
(sighing)
For all the good it does us.

Eula comes out on the balcony above. The two girls below look up at her.

EULA

Whooey. Clara, that baby brother of yours—I tell you he's like a five-year-old kid. Know what we was doin' in there? We was havin' a pillow fight. I hit him so hard I knocked the wind smack out of him. Hello, Agnes, sweety.

AGNES

Hello, Eula.

EULA

You sure do look calm and collected on this hot day.

AGNES

Well, I'm not. I'm damp and cranky.

EULA

I know what you mean. I'm goin' straight into a bubble bath myself . . . Agnes, you bring a beau by some one of these nights, and we'll cook us up a party.

JODY'S VOICE
(from within)
Eula! Where'd you disappear to!

EULA

If I'm not mistaken, that's my master's voice.

She waves and goes in. The two girls are alone. Agnes makes a face.

AGNES

Bring a beau by! My phone rang just one time last week, just one time, and this man with a deep beautiful voice says: "Can I interest you in the *Encyclopedia Brittanica*?"

CLARA

Come on, I'll give you a permanent and cheer you up.

AGNES

Clara, you've given me three permanents in the last six months. All my *ends* are split.
(pauses)
. . . It's unnervin', havin' all this time on my hands. I want to rush home and get dinner for some big handsome man, and put kids in a bathtub, and broil steak and crank ice cream, and think about what the night's goin' to bring . . .

(a cry)
Why aren't there enough men to go around?

CLARA
(dryly)
Oh, there's no shortage—except of the right kind.

AGNES
I'm not fussy on that subject!

CLARA
(humorously)
Neither am I.

AGNES
Tell me just one thing. Have you ever—in your whole life—been proposed to?

CLARA
(quietly)
Yes, I have.

AGNES
(incredulous)
And you let 'em go?

CLARA
No, I didn't let them go. I watched them get scared off . . .

A slight silence.

AGNES
Speakin' of your father, when's that august personage comin' home?

CLARA
Tomorrow. And the forecast is: storm and thunder.

The record starts up again in the room above.

AGNES
Come on over to my house for supper. Alan's been askin' about you. He's sick in bed, bein' fed milk puddin', all dreamy with temperature and enjoyin' himself. I'd give something to know what goes on in my brother's temperature dreams . . . I *know* what goes on in mine . . .

MED. SHOT—BEN QUICK—DAY
He turns into the walk approaching the house and pauses a moment to examine it. It is a large white mansion without elegance, but with a comfortable, lived-in look, surrounded by lush, beautiful grounds and a view of the river.

MED. SHOT—LAWN—DAY
Agnes sits up suddenly, looking over Clara's head. Her eyes light up.

> AGNES
>
> Don't swivel around—but there's someone comin'—someone young . . .

> CLARA
>
> It's probably a sewing machine salesman . . .

> AGNES
> *(intensely)*
>
> Even if it is—don't say No right off. Let's at least talk to him.

Ben approaches and pauses before them, smiling at the girls.

> BEN
> *(cheerfully)*
>
> Fine, warm day, isn't it, ladies?

> AGNES
>
> Yes, indeed! Pretty as a picture!

> BEN
>
> You look like two butterflies, lit on the grass.

Clara has risen at the sound of his voice. Now she looks at him coolly.

> BEN
>
> Hello again, Miss Clara.

> CLARA
> *(quietly)*
>
> If it's work you want, see the foreman at the gin. If it's food, they'll take care of you around at the back.

> BEN
> *(easily)*
>
> Why, you just haven't hit on it yet, lady. What I want now is the man of the house.

Clara opens the screen door and calls:

> CLARA

Lucius.

LUCIUS is the elderly colored servant. He comes out into the sunlight.

> LUCIUS

I left strawberry jam cookin', Miss Clara. What is it?

> CLARA

Tell Mister Jody there's a—
> *(slight pause)*
—a person here to see him.

Lucius motions Ben inside. But Ben lingers another moment.

> BEN
> *(to Clara, dryly)*

You could have said "gentleman" with the same amount of wind.

He goes inside. The two girls are alone again.

> AGNES
> *(amazed)*

Where did you find *him*?

> CLARA

Out on the road. I gave him a lift this morning.

> AGNES

Why'd you have to go and be so unfriendly?

> CLARA
> *(quietly)*

The last, desperate resort is strangers, Agnes. We haven't come to that yet.

> AGNES
> *(wildly)*

Oh, haven't we just! You want to hear a cold, clinical fact? Every single girl we went to Normal School with is married and pregnant or about to be. While I'm in residence with my mother and brother, and you're still occupyin' the bedroom you had when you were thirteen! I don't know about you, Clara, but I know what's makin' *me* nervous.

CLARA
(humorously)
Don't throw in the towel, Agnes, dear. Those tranquilizer
pills may see us through yet.

Agnes sighs.

INT. ENTRY HALL—VARNER HOME—DAY
*Ben stands looking with interest at the vast sweep of marble and mirror and
winding staircase. After a moment Jody comes down the stairs toward him,
rumpled and sweating. The two men, of an age, take a moment to size one
another up.*

There is a new record on now, a ballad, a male voice crooning a love lyric.

BEN
You Varner?

JODY
I'm one Varner.
(calls upstairs irritably)
Turn that thing off, Eula!
(to Ben)
What can I do for you?

BEN
My name is Quick. I heard you got a farm to rent.

JODY
(calling again)
Eula, you hear me! I'll come up there and kick that thing
in!

The music goes off immediately.

JODY
How much family you got?

BEN
You're looking at it.

JODY
A man usually puts six, seven hands in the field . . .

BEN
One is all you'll get from me.

Eula comes out on the landing above.

> EULA
> *(petulantly)*
> Jody, you got the store to talk business in . . .
> *(recognizes Ben; a large smile)*
> For heaven's sake, it's our *passenger.*

> BEN
> Howdy, ma'am.

> EULA
> Hello, yourself.

> JODY
> Here now! You two know each other? How come?

> EULA
> The how come is: Clara and I obliged him with a ride when
> his car broke down.

> JODY
> Well, get out of here. We're talkin'.

*Eula smiles at Ben and goes. Jody is a little more narrow with the stranger
now.*

> JODY
> What rent are you aimin' to pay?

> BEN
> What do you rent for?

> JODY
> Half your crop. Furnish out of my store. No cash.

> BEN
> I see. Food and tobacco at *your* prices. That makes the
> dollar worth about six bits.

> JODY
> Take it or leave it.

> BEN
> *(nodding)*
> I'll take it.

He turns and goes toward the front door. Lucius holds the door open for him. And then Lucius' eyes widen in dismay.

WHAT LUCIUS SEES—DAY
As Ben walks across the rug, he leaves behind wide, wet, muddy bootprints.

MED. SHOT—AT THE DOOR—BEN AND LUCIUS—DAY
As Ben goes out, Lucius speaks to him angrily.

> LUCIUS
> Mister, you sure do leave your calling card.

Ben smiles enigmatically and goes down the steps, sauntering along the walk away from the house.

EXT. MOVING SHOT—CLARA AND JEWEL—DAY
Taking a short cut through a cotton field, Clara walks swiftly. Behind her comes JEWEL, a little colored boy, carrying the soiled rug in a roll on his shoulders.

They approach a sagging, broken-backed cabin set in its inevitable treeless and grassless plot, weathered to the color of an old beehive.

EXT. THE CABIN—DAY
Ben Quick sits against the front door of his cabin, a large dripping chunk of watermelon in his hand, spitting out the seeds. As Clara and Jewel approach, Ben grins lazily.

> BEN
> Summertime—when the living is easy . . .

> CLARA
> *(pointedly)*
> When do you start work?

> BEN
> Lady, I never move and work in the same day.

She takes the rug from Jewel and unrolls it before Ben.

> CLARA
> My father's coming home tomorrow. He sets quite a value on this rug. You tracked it—you clean it.

> BEN
> *(smiling)*
> Lots of fuss about a rug, lady. If it's the rug that's bothering you.

> CLARA
> *(coolly)*

What else would it be?

> BEN

Well, now, you correct me if I'm wrong—but I have a feeling I rile you. Me being mean and dirty and all . . .

> CLARA
> *(evenly)*

Mister Quick, you're being personal with me, so I'll be personal with you. I've spent my whole life around men who push and shout and shove and think they can make anything happen just by being aggressive . . . and I'm not anxious to have another one around the place.

> BEN

Miss Clara, you slam a door in a man's face before he even knocks on it.

> CLARA
> *(slight pause)*

Please have the rug at the house by six.

She turns to go. But Jewel hangs back wistfully, looking at the fruit in Ben's hands. Ben breaks off a chunk and hands it to the little colored boy. Happy, Jewel trots after Clara. She looks down at the child with a slight smile.

> CLARA

Don't swallow the seeds.

They go back through the meadow. Ben remains where he is, relaxed, spitting seeds.

INT. AMBULANCE—MOVING SHOT—DAY
Black, hearse-like, its red lights blinking, its siren blasting the still air, it comes roaring into Frenchman's Bend. VARNER sits up front, riding with the DRIVER, resplendent in his bright red hospital bathrobe.

He is a huge man, powerful by virtue of his size and his immense energy, his gargantuan appetite for life. Shrewd, secret, merry, his hair more red than grey, he leans out the open window, grinning widely, enjoying the openmouthed townspeople scurrying out of the way of the racket.

The ambulance makes a complete circuit of the town square, passing Varner's Hardware Store, then the elegant little Public Library, then the Joy Movie Theater, and finally screeches past the General Store. And all the while Varner leans out the open window and laughs.

EXT. COURTHOUSE—DAY
The locals have looked up with interest. Lounging under the shade tree, Armistead turns to Ratliff and the others.

ARMISTEAD
Varner's home.

WILK
He don't look very peak-ed.

HOUSTIN
Anybody know what they cut out of him in that hospital?

RATLIFF
You can bet it wasn't his pocket-book . . .

The ambulance has disappeared, its siren still howling.

EXT. LITTLEJOHN'S HOTEL—DAY
It is a pleasant, old-fashioned building: a sign nailed to a shade tree reads, "ROOMS AND BOARD." A few drummers and livestock traders take their ease on the veranda; adjoining is a livery barn and a corral.

The ambulance pulls up and Varner pounds on the horn imperiously. MINNIE LITTLEJOHN, blonde and opulent, comes out on the porch of her hotel.

MINNIE
Is that you, Varner?

VARNER
You got any doubts, come closer!

She comes down the steps with a broad smile; he heaves himself out of the ambulance and catches her in his arms.

VARNER
Well, now, this is more like the land of the *livin'.*
(hugging her)
You're a little fatter and a little blonder—and a little more welcome than when I went away.

MINNIE

I understand they cut and stitched you. Anything *left* of you worth havin'?

VARNER

You put eight, ten cans of beer on ice, and wait and see. I'll be back later.

He jounces back into his seat and slams the door.

INT. AMBULANCE—DAY
The driver has watched the embrace with an open mouth. Varner looks at him smugly.

VARNER

These white hairs fooled you, didn't they, boy?

DRIVER

Yes, sir.

VARNER

Drive on!

EXT. ROAD—AMBULANCE—DAY
Again the siren screams. A flock of goats scurry frantically out of the way. The huge vehicle rocks through the village.

EXT. VERANDA—VARNER HOME—DAY
Lucius runs forward to take his bags as Varner mounts the steps of his porch.

LUCIUS

Welcome, Mister Will—welcome to your home.

VARNER

Lucius, I feel I'm back where I belong—in your capable hands again.

Lucius smiles and goes into the house. Varner turns to his family. Eula is elaborately dressed, glittering with earrings, curled and perfumed—she throws herself into his arms. He enfolds her in a great bear hug.

VARNER

You're dressed to beat all hell, girl.

EULA

In honor of you.

VARNER

Well, this is the kind of homecomin' I was hopin' for. For three calendar months I ain't smelled nothin' but the starch of nurses' uniforms.

(kisses her loud and smacking on the mouth)

Aah, that's what I like. The touch of a real woman. Bones with some coverin' on 'em.

He gives her a pat and puts her away from him. He turns to squint at Jody. Despite himself, his son goes white under the gaze.

JODY

Hello there, Papa.

VARNER

(sardonically)

Well, well. There's a fulsome greeting. There's a hallelujah chorus. Not exactly what you call dancin' in the streets, but adequate. Not exactly a son pinin' for his daddy, but simple and *di*-rect.

EULA

He *said* hello, didn't he?

CLARA

Is it possible for us to get through the opening ceremonies without civil war?

Varner's eyes flicker over to her.

VARNER

I'll be comin' to you in a minute.

CLARA

(not intimidated, quietly)

I know you will, Papa.

EULA

Jody's been an absolute, livin' doll while you been gone, Papa!

VARNER

I'd call that a glowin' recommendation—except that I just had a look around in town.

(to Jody again)

Have we retired? Have we left business? Are we livin' off of income? I saw one dead-asleep clerk keepin' store. No gin goin'.

JODY

Things may have slacked off a little bit today because I was home seein' to your arrival. But we done all right. You can look at the books.

VARNER

Why, now, I intend to. I'm goin' to crawl over them books like a fly over flypaper.

Lucius comes out momentarily with a tray and Varner helps himself to a long drink. He wipes off his mouth and then looks at Jody thoughtfully.

VARNER

Yes, I'm feelin' better—and thank you for your kind inquiries as to my health.

(pauses, looking at his son)

They gutted me down there in Jefferson. They took out every organ they thought I could spare. But they didn't pare down my spirit none.

Another pause. Clara looks at Varner brightly.

CLARA

Next?

VARNER

(turns to her slowly)

All right. You're on.

CLARA

What would you like to know, Papa?

VARNER

Are you fixin' to get yourself known as the best-lookin' old maid in the county or have you seen any young people? Have any young people seen you? Have you been to any parties, picnics, church bazaars? Any raffles, any barbecues, any hoedowns? Have you mingled? Have you mixed? Or did you keep to your room readin' poetry all this time?

CLARA
(tart)
I hope this doesn't come as any shock to your nervous system, Papa, but when you're not here I do what I want to.

VARNER
Well, I'm back!

CLARA
Welcome home.

He turns abruptly and goes into the house. Jody follows heavily after a moment.

INT. VARNER'S ROOM—DAY
A combination bedroom and study, full of litter, like the lair of an old lion. Varner peels off his robe, exposing a chest of bushy white hair. He examines his chin in a mirror, rummages in a closet for clothes, begins to dress. Jody enters and stands watching him quietly in the background.

JODY
(slowly)
You don't give me my respect in front of my wife . . .

VARNER
You got a business too, Jody. How about a little respect for that?
(pauses)
It's no use. You and me just don't talk the same language. It's what gives us our aches and our pains . . . Now me, I didn't lay flat on my back in that hospital. I wheeled and dealed. What about you?

JODY
May wasn't so good. June and July made up for 'em though.

VARNER
That's to be expected.

JODY
I moved out all that farm equipment. We're fresh out of inventory.

VARNER
Including that old tractor? The one that doesn't go uphill?

JODY

Including that . . . I rented off the tenant farm nobody
around here would have, and a fellow come down from
Boston, Massachusetts. He bought a lot of land and built a
big fence around it. He wanted to start a goat ranch. Only
he plumb ran out of goats and went bust—so, Papa, you
now got two thousand acres more of good grassland.

VARNER

Well, it seems you ain't been sittin' on your spine altogether.
How'd you rent that farm off?

JODY

On shares. I had a little trouble with the man. Penalized
him thirty bushels of corn.

VARNER

Good. We're already ahead of the game. What's the name
of this poor unfortunate?

JODY

Fellow name of Quick.

Varner stares at him incredulously.

VARNER

Quick? Ben Quick?

JODY

From out west . . .

VARNER
(suddenly raging)

You knuckle-headed fool. You empty-headed yokel.

JODY
(blanching)

What're you callin' me names for?

VARNER

Quick! Don't you keep abreast of anything but Eula? Don't
you know what Quick means in this county? *Hell fire!*
Ashes and char! Flame follows that man around like a dog!
He's a barn burner!

JODY
(white-faced)
I *never* do anything right, do I?

VARNER
Not to my immediate recollection!

JODY
You want to hear something? I sweat around you. All those months you were away in the hospital, I was *dry*. Now I'm sweatin' again.

VARNER
I can't stop to analyze you or listen to your emotional problems. I'm in a hurry. You started something with Mister Ben Quick and I got to finish it—before this house of mine goes up in smoke!

Varner goes out quickly. Jody remains behind in the room, trembling.

EXT. THE CABIN—DAY
Ben puts down the tools and comes forward to greet the stranger.

BEN
Howdy.

VARNER
Howdy. I'm Varner.

BEN
Already met one Varner.

VARNER
I'm the other. Just thought I'd drive by and see what your plans were.

BEN
The cabin isn't fit for hogs. But I can make out with it.

VARNER
(very friendly)
We can discuss that. Because I aim for us to get along.
(pauses)
I seem to have heard somewhere that you've had a little trouble with landlords. Trouble that might have been serious. That might have needed the help of the fire department.

                              BEN
                             (flat)
If you're scared of me, mister, why don't you come out and
say so?

                            VARNER
Now why should I be scared of you, son?

                              BEN
                            (gently)
Because I've got a reputation for being a dangerous man.

                            VARNER
You're a *young* dangerous man. But I'm an old one.
                            (pauses)
Allow me to introduce myself. I'm chief man in this county.
I'm Justice of the Peace and election commissioner. I'm a
farmer, a money-lender, and a veterinarian. I own the store
and the cotton gin and the grist mill and the blacksmith
shop, and it's considered bad luck for a man of the neigh-
borhood to do his trading or gin his cotton or grind his meal
or shoe his stock anywhere else.
                            (smiles)
That's who I am.

                              BEN
                            (softly)
You talk a lot.

                            VARNER
Yes, I do, son, and I'm goin' to add one more fact to this
conversation. If anything at all should happen to take fire
durin' your stay here, I'd have to take steps with you. I got
me a jail I built just last year down in my courthouse, and I
never heard of the words *habeas corpus*.
                  (a sudden, dangerous edge)
You'd *rot*.

                              BEN
                            (calmly)
A smart man would give me a job.

                            VARNER
You're already working for me.

BEN
(gesturing)
None of this weed-scratching. I'm talking about a job that'll
give me a white shirt and a black tie and three squares.
You've got a place in the store and a couple of other spots
where you could use me.
(smiling)
And you'd be writing a fire insurance policy into the bargain.

VARNER
(as he starts to leave)
I'll give it some thought.

Ben shakes his head; his voice is flat.

BEN
Yes or no, mister. Nothing in between.

VARNER
You're mighty bushy-tailed for a beginner.

BEN
I'm in a hurry.

VARNER
Won't do you no good. Around here, the job at the top is
already taken.

BEN
Yeah, but like you said—you're an old man.

VARNER
I am that. Keep it in mind and be respectful.

BEN
(mocking him)
Yes, *sir*, Mister Varner. Now who do I have to kill?

Varner smiles, secretly delighted with him.

VARNER
Well, we won't start right off with murder. I just got handed
thirty Texas ponies on a foreclosure. You dispose of 'em for
me at a reasonable profit, and you're in business.

And with this, Varner drives off.

EXT. STEWART'S GARDEN—DAY
Lovely, manicured grounds surround the charming old house. ALAN STEW-ART is in a lounge on the lawn; he is a man with a slim, patrician face, weary, pale from his illness.

Clara turns away from the gate where she has been standing and smiles at him.

CLARA
There's a nice breeze from the river, Alan . . .

ALAN
Everything nice comes with you—hot broth and a cool breeze from the river.

She sits on the lounge beside him.

ALAN
How's your school?

CLARA
(smiling)
You mean that free-for-all I run in town? Those thirty-five young hellions making their last stand against me? Well, it's not exactly a summer on the Riviera . . .

ALAN
It's unnatural to keep kids in school in the summer.

CLARA
They have to help with the crops in the fall—so some place along the line they've got to learn to read and write. I don't have much hope—but maybe I've got a young poet or a young painter cooped up down there.
(pauses, looking around)
Alan, I love this place. Grace and dignity and beautiful things left undisturbed—everything the way it was a hundred years ago.

ALAN
Most people say I'm fighting the twentieth century . . .
(pauses)
I suppose I should sell this land, or put it to corn and cotton . . . and go out and take a job, like everybody else. But I

wouldn't be any good at it. I'd hate it—and make a mess of
it.

CLARA

Then don't do it. There are enough hustlers running around
here as is. You stand for something. Hold on to it.

ALAN

Your father refers to me as decayed gentry.

CLARA

He's positively green with envy. Listen here. He'd give
anything to have what you have. Wouldn't he just like your
shine and polish. Yes, he's put up the billboards and the gas
stations and the neon signs, but quality is the one thing he
can't buy—and he knows it.

ALAN

He *has* quality—in you.

CLARA
(smiling)

That's what I came through this dusty summer day to hear.
(lightly)
I want you to be hale and hearty again. I want you to be
your gallant and courtly self again, and come calling on me.

ALAN

Very soon.

CLARA
(teasing)

You better. Girls get fidgety and talked about and looked at
sideways whcn they don't have gentlemen callers.
(pauses)
I've missed you.

She leans over suddenly and kisses him. Then she looks up at him brightly.

*He reaches for her and catches her hands. At that moment MRS. STEWART
walks into the scene.*

MRS. STEWART

That boy's temperature's been hoverin' between a hundred
and a hundred and two-tenths for three days—so none of that!

CLARA
(a little flustered)
I just brought over some of Lucius's soup . . .

MRS. STEWART
Oh, he won't eat a *bite* I don't cook. Now I'm goin' to hustle you right along, because he's long, long past his nap time.

CLARA
(gaily)
Very well, Mrs. Stewart. I'll give up the field—for now. Goodbye, Allan . . .

He waves at her. She goes. Mrs. Stewart picks up Clara's little jar of soup, looks at it critically, and goes into the house. Alan turns over wearily on his side; he turns on his portable radio. The garden fills with the music of Brahms.

EXT. CORRAL—DAY
The flock of ponies pound endlessly around in the corral, which lies just behind Littlejohn's Hotel. The horses are calico-coated, small-bodied, with delicate legs and pink faces in which their mismatched eyes roll wild and flashing. Dust rises like powder in the corral as they gallop savagely, gaudy, wild as deer, deadly as rattlesnakes.

WIDEN ANGLE—DAY
Ben Quick and Will Varner stand together against the fence, watching. Ben is appalled by the sight of the animals.

BEN
You old fake, they're horses out of hell!

VARNER
(grinning)
That's right.

BEN
Those ponies have never had a rope on 'em. You didn't tell me they were wild!

VARNER
Knowin' that gives you the edge over everybody else, don't it?

Varner pats him on the back, amused, and leaves him, walking toward the hotel. He looks about shrewdly as he goes.

FULL SHOT—THE YARD—DAY
There is a holiday feeling in the air, the excitement of a gala. Tethered wagons and riding horses and mules and trucks extend from the corral gate to Varner's store in the distance, and there are fifty men standing along the fence, examining the ponies.

Ben Quick stands apart, leaning against a post, his hands on his hips, staring at the merchandise he has promised to sell.

MED. SHOT—PORCH OF THE HOTEL—DAY
as Varner comes up the steps. Minnie waits for him in a wicker armchair, a bucket at her feet full of ice chunks and cold bottles of beer. Varner sits beside her. They watch the activity in the corral from their vantage point.

VARNER
Minnie Littlejohn, I'm getting thirsty again.

MINNIE
Since when you been in the horseflesh business, Will?

He uncaps a bottle of beer and drinks deeply. He smiles at her.

VARNER
That ain't no kind of business. What you're watchin' is a plain old-fashioned swindle. Of course, I ain't involved in it—directly.

MINNIE
You mean you hired that boy out there to fleece 'em.

VARNER
(thoughtfully)
Minnie, to tell you the truth . . . I don't quite know why I hired that boy. But I aim to find out.

EXT. THE CORRAL—DAY
Still the ponies wheel, a kaleidoscopic maelstrom of long teeth and wild eyes and slashing feet.

EXT. LANE BEFORE THE CORRAL—DAY
Clara drives slowly through the narrow, choked lane in the huge Cadillac. She blows her horn once or twice, but the press of teams and wagons soon

brings her to a halt—she is caught in the snarl of traffic. She gets out of the car, then climbs up on the wide, sloping hood to see better.

EXT. THE CORRAL—FEATURING BEN—DAY
One of the ponies crosses the lot at top speed and goes into the fence without any pause whatsoever. The wire gives, recovers, and slams the horse to the earth, where it lies for a moment, glaring, its legs still galloping in air. It scrambles up without having ceased to gallop and crosses the lot and roars into the opposite fence, and is slammed again to earth. The frenzy sends the others whipping and whirling about the lot like dizzy fish in a bowl.

Ben looks around almost helplessly. His eye catches that of Varner, seated on the porch in the background.

MED. SHOT—VARNER—DAY
He raises his beer bottle and toasts Ben sardonically.

EXT. CORRAL—DAY
Ben nods back thoughtfully. Then he addresses the crowd.

> BEN
> Okay, folks. Let's gather around. Let's move in here . . . I heard what you had to say about these horses, Mr. Armistead, and all I can tell you is I wouldn't hesitate to put my own sister on one of them. If I had a sister.

He suddenly singles Clara out with a brazen grin.

> BEN
> You there, Miss Clara. How'd you like to be the proud owner of one of these pretty little ponies?
> *(she does not answer)*
> If I'm not mistaken, you've got No written all over your face. But just stop and think a minute. You can pack yourself a picnic basket and follow some woodsy trail.
> *(brashly)*
> You can ride off steam and bad temper, if you happen to be afflicted that way. And if you see a young fellow along the way who takes your eye, you can put him up behind you and ride double. What's your answer, Miss Clara?

> CLARA
> *(dryly)*
> You were right the first time, Mister Quick. I have No written all over my face.

A chuckle of appreciation through the crowd.

> BEN
>
> That doesn't slow me down any, folks. Lots of women say No when they mean Yes.

Laughter from the crowd. He has swung them back to him. He begins to clap his hands for punctuation; his voice is lilting, his bravado catches them up:

> BEN
>
> The man that buys one will get the best piece of horseflesh he ever forked or drove for the money. Naturally they got spirit—I'm not selling crowbait. Come now, boys. Let's go, boys. Who's going to start her off with a bid?

A MAN speaks up:

> MAN
>
> I'll tell you what I'll do. I'll give you ten dollars for that there fiddle-head.

> BEN
>
> Ten dollars? You couldn't buy that much *dynamite* for just ten dollars. There isn't one of them can't do a mile in three minutes. Turn them into pasture and they'll board themselves. Work them like hell all day and every time you think about it. Lay them over the head with a single-tree and after a couple of days every jack rabbit one of them will be so tame you'll have to put them out of the house at night like a *cat*.

EXT. MINNIE'S PORCH—THE HORSE SALE IN BACKGROUND—DAY

Varner and Minnie are still seated side by side. There is a row of empty beer bottles at their feet now. Minnie is tiddly.

> MINNIE
> *(loudly)*
>
> Buzz, buzz, buzz, buzz!

> VARNER
> *(smiling at her)*
>
> What's the matter with you, Minnie?

> MINNIE
>
> I got a hum in my blood. Feel like I swallowed a bee.

                    VARNER
You swallowed five bottles of beer out in the hot sun, is
what you swallowed.

EXT. THE CORRAL—DAY
The auction continues.

                    BEN
Who's gonna give me fifteen dollars for that fiddle-head?

                    ARMISTEAD
You seem to know something about animals. I'll give fifteen.

PETE, Armistead's son, cheers his father on.

                    PETE
That's the way, Pa!

                    ARMISTEAD
Shut up, boy.

                    BEN
                    (loudly)
Who'll make it twenty?
                    (wiping his brow)
Who'll say seventeen-fifty?

EXT. MINNIE'S PORCH—DAY
Varner and Minnie continue their discussion.

                    MINNIE
                    (suddenly)
Kiss me, Will!

                    VARNER
                    (a bit uncomfortably)
I got a lot of friends and associates out there, Minnie.

                    MINNIE
I'm your friend. I'm your associate. And I *have* been for ten
years, Will. So far this summer I've put up twenty-two jars
of pick-a-lilly and I put a corn beef down in a crock—and I
ask myself: Where's it all goin' to end, Minnie?

                    VARNER
It's gonna end with me eating a corned beef. You know I'm
partial to it.

MINNIE

At midnight suppers, after you've come sneakin' up the back stairs. I want to serve it to you at six o'clock out here.

VARNER
(alarmed)

What are you sayin', woman?

MINNIE

I'm sayin' I've laid plans, Will. Matrimonial plans.

VARNER

I haven't asked you!

MINNIE
(firmly)

Well, I'm just goin' to overlook that. My married sister in Tallahassee is puttin' some hand-crocheted lace on some Piquot sheets for me. And I'm sendin' away for some flatware with the initial "V" on it.

VARNER

Minnie, I'm sixty years old!

MINNIE

Ain't no use your tryin' to tell me you're too old, because I happen to be in a position to deny it.

EXT. CORRAL—DAY
The horse sale is over. Ben slides off the post into the midst of the farmers, stuffing the final roll of bills into an already bulging pocket.

BEN
(cheerfully)

Thank you, boys, thank you kindly. Remember what I told you about busting those ponies over the head now and then until they get used to you. You won't have any trouble with them then.

WILK
(uncertainly)

Is that all there is to it? Do they belong to us now?

BEN

That's it. Take a piece of rope and go on in and take the one that's yours.

He walks away.

> **WILK**
> *(calling to the others)*
> We'll need rope! Get some rope!

EXT. IN THE LANE—DAY
Ben pauses a moment beside Clara. He smiles at her.

> **BEN**
> You're not much of a prospect, Miss Clara.

> **CLARA**
> You don't need my money. You've got everybody else's.

> **BEN**
> It's the hold-out that challenges me.

> **CLARA**
> Mister Quick, the last time I parted with my money to a pitchman, I was twelve years old.

> **BEN**
> *(grinning)*
> And nobody's ever taken you since, huh?

> **CLARA**
> And nobody's going to, Mister Quick.

> **BEN**
> Life's very long and full of salesmanship, Miss Clara. You might buy something yet.

He nods at her and goes on. She looks after him.

EXT. CORRAL—DAY
The farmers now have a length of rope apiece. They enter the corral in a bunch, each going toward his own pony, to tie it and claim it. They enter slowly, cautiously, huddled together in fear of the snorting animals. And the last man in swings the gate only partially behind him—he forgets to lock it.

The next instant all is disaster. The farmers whirl suddenly and run before a gaudy vomit of long wild faces and splotched chests; they are overwhelmed and scattered and flung sprawling aside by an explosion of ponies.

Armistead falls flat on the ground over his son Pete, to cover the boy from the forest of striking hooves.

Straight to the open gate the eruption of horses churns, carrying the gate with them, taking even the upright with its hinges. Women cry, gather up their skirts, and run; men crawl under wagons and trucks; children shinny up trees. The horses clatter among the teams and wagons that choke the lane, sending mules plunging, snapping hitch-reins and wagon tongues.

Clara scurries to the top of her car, starts sliding down again; a passing man heaves her back up.

EXT. CORRAL—DAY
The whole inextricable mass of Texas ponies eddy and divide, one half going down the lane, the other making for the open road and the open countryside.

Behind them the farmers pound in their hobnailed boots and the dusk resounds to their cries:

> ARMISTEAD
There goes mine!

> HOUSTIN'S SON
Look out, Paw!

> WILK
There's yours!

> McCASLIN
Hey—catch mine!

> PEABODY
Halloo, halloo!

EXT. LITTLEJOHN PORCH—DAY
Ben, Varner, and Minnie duck away as one wild maverick plunges through the yard, runs up the front steps, crashes on the wooden veranda, and vanishes, galloping, through the front door.

> MINNIE
Get out of my hotel!

She runs in, snatching up a broom. A woman screams from within.

A deep, rumbling chord crashes out on a piano inside.

> VARNER
> *(grinning)*
That's a musical hoss there . . .

FULL SHOT—THE TOWN—DAY
Two loose horses, followed close by their sweating owners, gallop through the center of the village, across the courthouse lawn, down the sidewalk in front of the Joy Movie Theater, and at last out to open country beyond.

EXT. LITTLEJOHN PORCH—DAY
Ben, Varner, and Minnie are together on the porch, listening to the frantic cries in the night.

                    VARNER
They'll go on all night—tryin' to catch them rabbits.
                    (turns to Ben)
You got something belongs to me.

Ben nods and empties out his pockets.

                    BEN
You're no better than a crook.

                    VARNER
And you're no better than a con man, if you can sell my crooked merchandise.

                    BEN
Never mind name calling. Where's my share?

                    VARNER
Oh, I've got something for you.
                    (heaves himself up)
Come along.

He goes down the steps. Ben follows.

FULL SHOT—EDGE OF TOWN—DAY
The air is still filled with faint sounds—shouts thin and distant, the thunder of hooves here and there, on wooden bridges and on dirt roads, more shouts faint and thin and earnest and clear as bells, the entire landscape full of them:

                    VOICE
Whooey!

                    SECOND VOICE
Head him!

                    THIRD VOICE
There goes mine!

VOICE

Whooey!

EXT. FRENCHMAN'S PLACE—DAY

Ben and Varner stand together in the gutted shell of a once enormous plantation, with its fallen stables and slave quarters, its garden wild with weeds. Floors and posts have long since been carried away and chopped up for firewood; mold and decay are over everything. Varner looks about soberly.

VARNER

The man who built this place—his name's forgotten. This was his dream and his pride—now it's dust. Must be a moral there somewhere.

BEN

Looks like that's about *all* there is.

VARNER

We got us a legend about this place. It's said that money was buried somewhere on the grounds when Grant overran the country on his way to Vicksburg.

BEN

What's that got to do with me?

VARNER
(thoughtfully)
I've been watchin' you. I've seen your brass, I've seen your style, I've seen your push—and it's not too dissimilar from the way I operate. You've been here a couple of days and you've gone up an inch. That's because you listened to me. You *keep* listenin' to me—
(grins)
—and maybe, some day, in a burst of generosity, I'll give you this place.

BEN

Thanks for nothing. It's falling apart.

VARNER

Well, with your native shrewdness, you'll find a way of gettin' some good out of it.

                    BEN
                    (suddenly tough)
You've been making me a lot of promises. One day I'm
going to collect on 'em.

                    VARNER
                    (bland)
Sholy.

                    BEN
                    (flat)
I'm not just passing the time of day with you, mister!

                    VARNER
I'm well aware of that.
                    (claps him on the back)
Come and eat at the big house, son.

Ben nods. Varner is smiling at him.

INT. DINING ROOM—NIGHT
*The table is heavy with platters, candles, wine. Lucius serves the meal. Ben
Quick and Alan Stewart are the guests of the Varner family.*

*Varner presides at the head of the table. The French doors are open to the
warm air of night and the faint cries of the cheated farmers are still heard as
they chase horses, running in the moonlight after the clatter of hoofs. There is
a brief rapid thunder of hoofs on wooden planking.*

                    JODY
There's another one on the creek bridge.

                    VARNER
Those poor unfortunates are goin' to come out ahead on
them things after all. They'll get the money back in exercise
and relaxation. It's good for 'em. It stimulates their liver.

                    ALAN
                    (quietly)
They'll catch those horses.

                    VARNER
Maybe.

ALAN

They'll catch them—and they'll make good work teams out of them.

VARNER

You figure you know those redneck farmers better than me. I suppose that's because the Stewart family's been in these parts longer than the Varners.

CLARA
(gently)

About two hundred years.

BEN
(shakes his head)

That's a long time in one place.

ALAN

You don't believe in belonging to one place?

BEN

My family *moved*. Not that they wanted to. They were encouraged by the local citizens.

EULA

You a hunted man or something?

BEN
(smiling)

Something, Miss Eula.

JODY
(suspiciously)

I'd like to hear a Yes or No answer to that.

VARNER

Well, if he's hunted he ain't *caught*. That's good enough for me.
(raises the decanter)
Now who's drinkin' some more brandy?

He singles out Alan and fills his glass to the brim. Then he smiles at the man.

VARNER

You're partial to my brandy, ain't you, Alan? How many years you been drinkin' it? Five? Six?

ALAN

I've enjoyed your hospitality for a long time.

VARNER

Do you go to any other houses? I ask myself: Do we get the *major* part of your attention? Or are you brightenin' up *other* parlors in town?

CLARA
(angrily)

That's Alan's private business!

VARNER

Oh—Alan knows a friendly inquiry when he hears one. Don't you, Alan?

ALAN
(coolly)

When I hear one.

VARNER

Sho. Friendly inquiries never bothered no one . . . Well, then. Am I to understand that you stay pretty close to home, with your mother, when you're not here?

CLARA

Papa, I can't stand this!

Alan puts his hand over hers gently. He replies, his voice even.

ALAN

I think you've forgotten that my mother is a widow, Mister Varner. She relies very strongly on me.

VARNER
(snorting)

Widow, hell! Your old man ain't dead, he just disappeared. He just *wandered* off.

ALAN
(thinly)

The end result is the same. She's alone.

VARNER

No, she ain't! She's got you. She sure has you, Alan.

ALAN

I do my best.

VARNER
(slamming the table)
Not around *here*, you don't!

Clara closes her eyes in absolute misery. Jody snickers.

JODY

Huh-huh-huh.

Eula digs him sharply with her elbow. Varner sucks his teeth briefly and loudly, looking at his son.

VARNER

You seem to be enjoyin' my conversation, Jody. I'll direct a little bit of it at you.

JODY
(sullenly)
I didn't say nothin'.

VARNER

This Ben Quick here is my new clerk in the store—right along side of you. Same salary, same benefits.
(pauses)
That don't seem to strike you funny.

JODY
(quietly)
It don't.

VARNER

You can sleep late tomorrow—if you feel you can afford to.

Jody drinks off his glass. His eyes go slowly to Ben Quick. Their glances meet and hold.

Varner pushes back from the table and bellows:

VARNER

Outside, everybody—take the evenin' air!

He crooks his arm through Ben's and starts out. Jody follows unhappily, Eula pulling him. Alan and Clara linger behind.

CLARA
(suddenly intense)
I apologize for what we are!

ALAN
Don't, Clara. It isn't necessary.

CLARA
I wouldn't blame you if you left right now. Other young men have departed before you—with less reason than this.

ALAN
(smiling)
My people have stood off Indians and Yankees and carpet-baggers. The least they'd expect of me is to face up to a Varner.

CLARA
(also smiling)
All right. Then let's go out and have some more.

He offers her his arm. They go through the French doors.

EXT. THE VERANDA—NIGHT
The others sit in chairs with their feet up on the veranda rail, drinking coffee and brandy and smoking beneath the bug-swirled lamp. Alan and Clara take their places in a swing.

The shadows have lengthened; frogs and whippoorwills are noisy; fireflies dart in profusion.

And hidden in the bushes some distance below the veranda, a pack of wild young farm boys begin their evening entertainment.

BOYS
(calling)
Eula! Eula! Yoo-hoo-hoola!

EULA
(giggling)
Listen to that. If those young boys don't sound like a bunch of tomcats, yowlin' at the moon.

BOYS
Eula! Eula! Yoo-hoo-hoola!

> EULA

Isn't it terrible, the way they come prowlin' around here every night? It's like that in town, too. They follow me wherever I go.

> JODY
> *(angrily)*

Don't go anywhere, then! Stay put. Stay close to home!

> EULA

They're harmless, Jody. They're only sixteen, seventeen years old.

> JODY

You call that harmless!

Jody stands up suddenly and shouts into the night.

> JODY

You quit it out there or I'll pass among you with a shotgun!

> VARNER
> *(amused)*

Banshees!

> JODY
> *(incensed)*

Hitch your chair back, Eula! Get out of the light!

> VARNER

They don't have to *see* her. They can *smell* her.

Clara rises abruptly, going to the edge of the veranda, shouting out into the bushes.

> CLARA

Tom Shortly! V.K. Bookwright! Buddy Peabody! I *know* it's you out there! Stop it, now!
> *(turning back to the others)*

Somebody stop them!

Jody's chair crashes as he vaults over the veranda and leaps down into the darkness.

> JODY

I'll damn well stop them!

He is gone. Clara laughs self-consciously.

CLARA

It's a madhouse around here.

VARNER

They're just boys. Just healthy young animals.

She swings around to her father with an outburst.

CLARA

Are they hollering around anybody else's doorstep? Are they hiding in anybody else's garden? It's just *this* house! We're the ones who are always singled out!

VARNER
(smiling)

We're the ones who've got Eula.

CLARA

It's not her fault. It's yours. They come because they know you'll laugh, you'll think it's funny, no matter how crude, how vulgar!

VARNER

I was young myself once. *I* hid in the greenery and hooted and bellowed.

CLARA

I'm sure you did. You probably stayed longest and yelled loudest.

VARNER
(quietly)

Your momma listened.

She falls still. Ben is smiling at her. She looks away.

INT. VARNER'S STUDY—NIGHT
Ben and Varner are hunched over a grimy deck of cards, playing twenty-one for silver dollars.

VARNER

Black jack!

BEN

All right.
(watches his money scooped away)
Now let's deal off the top.

Varner looks at him slyly.

BEN

This the way you acquired your fortune? It's the way you're acquiring mine . . .

Varner snorts and deals. They play in silence a while.

MED. SHOT—THE SWING—NIGHT

A long silence. Clara and Alan sit alone in the swing. She leans back, bemused and dreamy.

CLARA

Those boys certainly make their desires plain. Calling and calling—as if Eula would just get up and follow them.
(*thoughtfully*)
I wonder what would happen if Eula *did* follow them?

ALAN
(*smiling*)
I imagine there'd be quite a romp.

CLARA
(*musing*)
Now why'd I go and make such a fuss about it? . . .

ALAN

Because it offended you.

CLARA

No, it didn't. There's the plain, unvarnished truth at last. You know, Alan, there's no sense in pretending girls don't think about sex. They do. You ought to hear some of the conversations between Agnes and me.

ALAN

I'd like to.

CLARA
(*with slight mockery*)
Nothing special about being anxious over your love life.
(*directly*)
I am about mine.

A silence. She moves restlessly.

CLARA

Oh dear! This is not at all the way I expected this conversation to go. I was going to sit on the swing here with you and let the moon shine on us and—just like those boys out there—let nature take its course . . .

Alan leans over to her, takes her face in his hands.

ALAN

Nature *is* taking its course with you. You're not the kind to be howled at and dragged off a porch into the bushes. You *are* a nice, quiet, self-contained girl, Clara.
(his face is very close)
And you'll see . . . everything you want is going to happen to you . . .

He kisses her gently.

INT. VARNER'S STUDY—NIGHT
A twelve-year-old black girl, ALICE, stands on the other side of the screen door, looking through it at Ben and Varner.

VARNER

Good evenin', Alice. You lookin' for me?

ALICE

Miss Minnie Littlejohn says: "Where are you?"

VARNER
(smiling)

Where am I, eh?

ALICE

Yes, sir. She says if you're not there in half an hour, the place'll be triple-locked against you.

VARNER

Triple-locked, eh? Well, you go back and tell Miss Littlejohn I'll be there when I'm there.

ALICE

I'll tell her.

She goes. Varner looks at Ben.

VARNER
It appears as if I have a late date.

He pauses, looking at Ben shrewdly.

VARNER
You married? You got a woman someplace?

BEN
I live single.

VARNER
You've known a few, though, haven't you?

BEN
(coolly)
My fair share. Deal.

Varner stops talking. They play.

EXT. VERANDA—NIGHT
It is later. Clara is curled up alone in the swing, rocking gently back and forth. She is abstracted, heavy with languor. Ben interrupts her reverie.

BEN
Your friend left early.

Her reply to his impudence is a long, cool stare.

CLARA
I was kissed goodnight, Mister Quick.

BEN
Kissed and left.
(smiling)
Me—I'd have stayed till sun-up.

CLARA
(sardonically)
My, aren't you reckless.

BEN
(coming closer)
Aren't you?

CLARA
(mocking)
No, I'm just skittish, Mister Quick. Just plain skittish.

BEN
(abruptly)
Well, I know an answer to that. Let's get in that old Cadillac car of yours and plough up the countryside. Let's go holler off a bridge good and loud.

CLARA
I think there's been enough commotion around here.

BEN
You want quiet? Then let's go find us a needle in a haystack.

CLARA
Those are all lovely, colorful suggestions, Mister Quick. But if I stood up to follow you, I'd hear the starch in my petticoat rustle—and I'd know I was out of character.

BEN
Get out of character, lady. Get *way* out.

CLARA
(slowly)
Sudden changes are not in my line.

BEN
You'll never know till you try.

CLARA
There's a volume of Jane Austen beside my bed—and a glass of hot milk that's getting cold . . .

BEN
You mean your friend wouldn't like it if you went off with me. The idea of you and me wouldn't go down, would it?

CLARA
(stiffly)
I don't want to discuss him with you.

BEN
Why not? I respect him. I admire his manners. I admire the speeches he makes. I admire the big house he lives in.

(grinning)

But if you're saving it all up for him, lady, you've got your account in the wrong bank.

CLARA

You can leave any time now.

BEN

Don't ask me twice.

And just as abruptly as that he goes.

She sits troubled, looking after him, slapping impatiently at a mosquito. Then she rises slowly, reluctantly, as if unwilling to end the night. She goes into the house.

INT. ENTRY HALL—NIGHT

She enters in the dim light, still moving slowly, wearily. She catches sight of herself in the great mirror and pauses, studying her reflection, her eyes large, questioning. Then she turns away and goes toward the stairs.

Varner's voice stops her.

VARNER'S VOICE

Clara!

The door to his study is open. She goes to him.

INT. VARNER'S STUDY—NIGHT

He sits sprawled in his chair, a big wreath of smoke around his head, watching her like a dour Buddha. She pauses in the entrance.

VARNER

Sit down.

She obeys, still abstracted, wrapped in her secret thoughts. He watches her.

VARNER

When did Alan leave?

CLARA

About ten . . .

VARNER

Early.

CLARA

He's been ill.

VARNER

Yeah.

They fall still. He watches her warily. She seems unaware of his scrutiny. Frogs, crickets, whippoorwills: the window is open to all the sounds of the night.

VARNER

You look kind of pale yourself.

CLARA

It's hot. I haven't been sleeping well . . .

VARNER

How old are you now, Clara?

CLARA
(thoughtfully)

Don't you know?

VARNER
(shrugging)

I keep a lot of figures in my head.

CLARA

Well, add these: I'm twenty-three.

VARNER

Your mother was eighteen when I married her. Just turned.

CLARA

Papa, are we going to talk about that again?

VARNER
(nodding slowly)

We are.

CLARA

You never look at me. My birthdays come and go, my life comes and goes—
(a little helplessly)
You know, I'm quite a lively, intelligent girl. Sometimes I even make people laugh. And yet, we don't seem to have any other conversation but this one.

VARNER
(shortly)

You're unmarried.

CLARA
You've pointed that out before.

A slight silence. He points to the veranda.

VARNER
What do you do out there, you and Alan?

CLARA
We talk.

VARNER
What gets said? Anything of importance?

CLARA
(smiling faintly)
He thinks I'm a nice, quiet, self-contained girl . . .

Varner stubs out his cigar with sudden violence.

VARNER
Well, that's not damn near enough!

He rises and prowls. He stops by the open window and speaks aloud as though to himself:

VARNER
Thousands of acres. Millions of seeds put down in the ground. And every year they come up, they bear. Life's goin' on out there—continuous, sure, inevitable.
(slowly)
Where's my crop? What follows me? What happens when I die?

CLARA
(quietly)
I expect you'll have the biggest funeral in the state of Mississippi.

VARNER
(evenly)
That don't scare me none—if there are a lot of Varners to mourn me.

CLARA
Jody and I will be there.

VARNER
(intensely)
Jody and you and your children and your children's children
will be there!

He is suddenly fierce with passion.

VARNER
A *line*, Clara. A long line. With my name. With my face
stamped on them. With my blood in their veins. That's how
I'm goin' to stay alive *forever*.

CLARA
(wryly)
All that?—from the two of us?

VARNER
(dangerously)
You think I'm jokin'? I'm not. You think I'm makin' merry
here? I'm not. Listen to me, Clara.

He comes and sits close to her, leaning to her, driving, emphatic, inexorable.

VARNER
If your blood is so delicate and frail that it calls out for
Alan—amen! So be it. Let it be Alan! I'll give you a big
weddin' and a New Orleans trousseau—and everybody, *everybody*, will come in their best and their finest. I'll build
you a house. I'll put money in Alan's account in the Jefferson First Trust Bank. But it's goin' to happen *now*. No
more *pussyfootin'*, missy. No more holdin' hands and
squeakin' that front porch swing back and forth. I've heard
that sound for six years.
(rises wrathfully)
Well, I'm not goin' to hear it any more. Go tell his momma
to let *go*. Tell her you're takin' over—'cause your daddy
says so, if you can't think of a better reason.
(pauses)
But if you get No for an answer, I tell you it's goin' to be
the other one!

She looks at him in horror.

CLARA

Which other one?

VARNER

That blue ribbon bull! That hand-grown, hand-picked, hand-selected-by-me fellow name of Quick.

CLARA
(whispering)
You can't mean him . . .

VARNER

Can't I? I'm goin' to get me some good, strong, strappin' men in this family. I'm goin' to feed iron into this family's veins. Varners and more Varners and still more Varners! Varners enough to infest the countryside. I'm goin' to see that happen before I die. I'm goin' to accomplish that. And it'll be by means of that Quick—that big, stud horse—he's the one who'll give 'em to me!

CLARA
(an outcry)
You'd sell me away like that! Just like that! Without caring what *I* want. What I *feel*. What I *am*.

VARNER
I ain't sellin' you. I'm *savin'* you.

CLARA
Is that what you tell yourself!

VARNER

You're goin' to give me grandsons, Clara. You can get 'em by way of Alan, or you can get 'em by way of that other one. But you're goin' to do it. Get that ring on your finger!

EXT. VARNER HOUSE—DAY
Jody dashes from the house, still dressing, buttoning his shirt and running.

EXT. SQUARE—MOVING SHOT—JODY RUNNING—DAY
He races into the square and starts across the street toward the store. A thick crowd of country people are already there, mingling on the gallery. Jody pauses panting beside Ratliff.

EXT. STORE—DAY

JODY

What's goin' on?

RATLIFF

They ain't come to do much buyin'—penny worth of candy, two cents worth of nails. They're here to look.

JODY

What at? We ain't runnin' no side show.

RATLIFF
(gently)

They come to look at the new man. Three days ago they never even knew his name—but in the future they're goin' to have to be dealin' with him for all the necessaries of livin' . . .

JODY

They'll deal with me! Like always!

He strides away from Ratliff and goes up the steps. He stops in the doorway.

INT. STORE—DAY

Ben is behind the counter in a white glazed shirt and a little black bow tie, cheerful and busy, just handing a customer change. The two young men look at one another for a long moment. In the background the locals crowd closer to stare through the open door and watch the meeting.

BEN
(pleasantly)

It's the early bird, Jody . . .

Jody clenches his hands furiously—but before he can speak MRS. HOUSTIN tugs at his sleeve. She is gaunt and work-worn, her voice is toneless.

MRS. HOUSTIN

Mister, my little chaps at home never had shoes last winter. We ain't got corn to feed the stock. Them thirty dollars my husband paid for that horse yesterday—which he ain't even seen since then—I earned sewing at night.

She stops, her thin hands folded in her apron. Jody shakes his head at the unfairness of it all:

JODY

Boy, if that ain't the limit. You get greased and fleeced— and then you come in here and lay it at my door.

He looks with a glint of triumph at Ben.

> JODY
>
> Trouble is we got an outsider here . . . don't know nothin',
> don't *care* nothin' about you and your worries. No, sir, he
> don't care about nothin' except advancin' himself.

> BEN
> *(dryly)*
>
> A lot of harsh things been said about me. And if I was to
> answer each and every one of 'em, it would take up too
> much of your valuable time, Missus.
> *(smiles)*
> So I'll just tell you, Missus, that you took your complaints
> to the wrong department. We're under new management.
> You got a thirty-dollar problem?
> *(rings the register, hands her some bills)*
> It's solved.

*She bobs her head at him; without a word she hurries out. Ben smiles
broadly at Jody.*

> BEN
>
> Good will. Nothing in the world like it.

> JODY
> *(raging)*
> You think you got a cozy nest here, don't you? Well, you
> ain't goin' to take over from me!

*Jody takes an angry step closer and then stops, the action interrupted by the
sound of a voice. It is Varner, outside, greeting the crowd.*

EXT. PORCH OF STORE—DAY

> VARNER
> . . . Well, gentlemen, off with the old and on with the new.
> It's the old shop, the old stand—it's just a new broom in it
> . . . Maybe you can't teach an old dog new tricks, but you
> can teach a new young willin' one anything. Just give him
> time—a penny on the waters pays interest when the flood
> turns . . .

Jody steps outside and confronts his father. The old man meets his gaze with a quizzical look. Jody is suddenly quiet and pale.

                              JODY
Thank you for your encouragement and kind support . . .

He goes down the steps, blundering, as if he cannot see where he is going. He marches away.

EXT. EULA'S UPSTAIRS VERANDA—DAY
Jody sprawls on the porch, looking moodily up at the sky.

Eula emerges from the bedroom behind him, shielding her face against the glare.

                              EULA
Jody, ain't you *ever* goin' to work again? You *always* goin' to be hangin' around? Honestly, I can't paint my nails or do my *hair* without havin' you hangin' around . . .
                            (pauses)
You take that Ben Quick. He's down at the store—he's workin'—he's sweatin'—he's where you *ought* to be.

                              JODY
                            (growling)
Who're you to tell me to work? You ain't *never* out of a chair. Only time I seen you break cover is when they're sweepin' or cleanin' the house, or callin' you to the dinner table.

                              EULA
                             (hurt)
You got no call to be insultin'. As your wife, I just don't want to see you get passed by that boy.

                              JODY
                         (staring at her)
One place he'll never pass me.

He rises slowly and walks toward her.

                              EULA
                           (wailing)
Jody, it's noon time!

He reaches for her. She pulls free.

EULA
Listen here. I'm goin' to busy myself *elsewhere—day* times anyway. I'm goin' to remove myself.
(suddenly)
I'll get me an education, that's what I'll do. Clara's been after me for months, sayin' it's never too late to learn . . .
(seriously)
I sure do wish you'd get yourself some other kind of recreation . . .

He leads her inside, kicks the door shut. The shutters are closed with a violent slam.

INT. SCHOOLROOM—NIGHT
A lamp is burning on the desk. Clara finishes scribbling her comments in the margin of the final essay.

The clock above her head shows nine. She rises and rubs her back ruefully. She puts out the lamp and goes.

EXT. MOVING SHOT—CLARA—NIGHT
She strolls slowly down the dusty main street of town. A light is burning in the store; as she passes she can see Ben Quick on a ladder, rearranging merchandise within. She goes on a few paces, then stops and looks curiously back at the store. She retraces her steps and goes in.

INT. STORE—NIGHT
Ben comes down the ladder as she enters. She glances about tentatively, sees his unfinished glass of beer on a table, his coat and tie thrown in a heap on a chair. Then she turns to him. She looks at him secretly, seeing him now in a new and dangerous frame of reference—Varner's stud horse. She watches him intently—though her words are casual.

CLARA
It's rather late to be keeping store . . .

BEN
I'm moving the cotton dresses down front, where the ladies can see them when they first come in.

CLARA
You seem to know a lot about women.

BEN
I know what makes them spend their money.

(pauses)
You come here to buy something, Miss Clara, or are you just shopping around?

CLARA
(disconcerted)
I was just passing . . .

BEN
It's a hot night. I've been drinking beer. You want some?

CLARA
No, thank you . . .

BEN
Got a sweet tooth? I can offer you rock candy, jawbreakers, licorice whips—I do a big business in licorice whips.
(she shakes her head; he smiles)
Outgrown 'em, eh?
(he looks over the shelves)
Spotted dimity, sun bonnets, hand cream, freckle remover, lilac water?
(she is still silent)
Just can't sell you, can I?

CLARA
May I have an aspirin, please? I've got a headache . . .

BEN
We've got all kinds of nostrums and remedies.

He pours her a glass of water, hands her a tablet. As she takes it he watches her speculatively.

BEN
I don't have headaches myself. That's because I don't have problems.

CLARA
Or scruples.

BEN
(slowly)
Not those, either.

CLARA

Well, I have both . . .

BEN

You've got a thin skin, is what you've got. The world belongs to the meat eaters. And if you've got to take it raw, take it raw.

CLARA

I couldn't live that way!

BEN

Well, now, Miss Clara, let's examine the way you do live. You drive that old Cadillac car around like it had wings, you teach school, you sit on your side porch with your skinny little friend drinking lemonade—and what's that, when you see the whole world going by paired up. You're twenty-three—those are the golden years—and you're being asked to play a waiting game. Well, why wait?
(coming nearer, smiling)
School's out. Night's fallen. The blinds are drawn. There's nobody here to see you if you make a mistake.
(quietly)
Put down your books, Miss Clara. I'm going to kiss you.

He reaches for her. Both her hands are clamped suddenly by his, both her wrists prisoners.

BEN

I'm going to show you how simple it is. You please me and I please you.

She slaps him on the cheek.

BEN

I'll tell you what's troubling you . . . It's all those boys calling for Eula every night—and Eula with her hair hanging down—and Jody chasing her with his shirt off—and your old man, at sixty, calling on his lady love . . .

She puts her arms around him suddenly, wild, distracted, amazed, and responds to him. Then she twists out of his arms savagely. Trembling, she cries:

CLARA

All right, I'm human. You've proved it.

BEN

Yes, ma'am. You're human, all right.

CLARA

Barn burner! Barn burner!

He steps back and stares at her. He is vulnerable at last, cold with anger. A long pause.

BEN

Well, you hit on it. I see my white shirt and my black tie and my Sunday manners didn't fool you for a minute. That's right, ma'am, I'm a menace to the countryside. All a man's got to do is look at me sideways, and his house goes up in fire. And here I am living right in the middle of your peaceable little town, right in your back yard, you might say. I guess that ought to keep you awake at night.

She turns and goes out swiftly. He wheels around in a fury and sweeps his fist along the counter—boxes and cans and bottles go crashing.

He stands a long while leaning against the counter, his face dark with anger. He pushes away at last. He snaps off the light and steps outside.

EXT. PORCH OF THE STORE—NIGHT
He rattles the door hard to make sure it is locked. And as he turns he finds Varner on the bench in the dark, sitting on his spine, legs crossed, cigar glowing, watching him.

VARNER

Anything you break you got to pay for.

BEN
(coldly)

What are you doing here?

VARNER

Taking the air.

BEN

You hired me to tend your store. I'm tending it. That doesn't need any supervision.

VARNER

I see you've been havin' a few words with my girl.

BEN

A few.

VARNER

And she don't cotton to you none, does she?

BEN

There's no love lost.

VARNER

Well, that don't have to slow you down.

He looks at Ben coolly.

VARNER

I've put you forth as a candidate.

BEN

What office have you got me running for?

Varner does not answer for a moment.

VARNER

I've opened a lot of doors for you. And you've passed through 'em. Now ask yourself why I've done it. Am I a senile old man? Am I a sentimental old fool? I am *not.*

BEN

All right. So?

VARNER

I'm a man with a purpose.

BEN

We all got some mission in life.

VARNER

Care to hear yours?

BEN
(evenly)

What do you think you'd like me to do—if you were able to make me do it?

> VARNER

Get married. Have sons.

> BEN

Well, I'll be damned . . .

> VARNER

There's every possibility of that—but before you are, you'll be married up in a church to my daughter Clara.

Ben shakes his head slowly. Varner watches with enjoyment.

> VARNER

Now that's the one you didn't figure, isn't it?

> BEN

That's the one . . .

> VARNER

Well. What do you say?

> BEN

I say . . . it's a mighty interesting notion . . .

> VARNER
> *(suddenly passionate)*

Notion! I'm talkin' about the establishment of my immortality. I'm talkin' about the survival of my family name!
> *(intensely)*

You want to put down roots! Move into the house. Live with us. Sleep under clean sheets. Study that skinny girl.

> BEN

What's in it for me?

> VARNER

Land and monies on the day of the weddin'. And more to come.

> BEN

What land? What monies? How *much* more?

> VARNER

We'll have a meetin' with my banker and my lawyer. You'll see for yourself.

BEN

I'll take that old Frenchman's ruin as a starter. Now. Tonight.

VARNER

I'll give it to you in writin'.

BEN
(nodding)

You do that.

Varner suddenly stands. He cries out exultantly:

VARNER

Hah! Don't tell me I picked the wrong man!
(grins wolfishly)
You and me got a deal, Ben Quick! Who says marriages are
made in heaven?

BEN
(quietly)

Hell wouldn't have this one.

Varner leans forward to peer at the boy. He is suddenly anxious.

VARNER

Don't mistake this girl. She's delicate. In her own way she's
fine. She has quality, like her mother before her, and it's as
close as you or I will ever come to it.

EXT. CABIN—DAY
*Ben emerges from his cabin, carrying his two suitcases, his banjo and bird
cage. His hands full, he kicks the door shut with his foot, but it swings open
again. He kicks once more, it swings back again. He kicks a third time and
the warped and splintered door rasps off its hinges and falls to the ground.
Ben shrugs. A nanny goat, in the front yard, wanders past him and puts its
head in the open door. Ben addresses the animal:*

BEN

Go right on in. It's all yours. I'm moving up in the world.

He turns and walks away.

FULL SHOT—COTTON FIELDS—DAY
*The cotton is now open and spilling into the fields. Cotton pickers go among
the bursting bolls, dragging long, partly filled sacks behind them. The air is*

hot and vivid. Wisps of cotton cling to roadside weeds, as after a summer snow; the air is full of lint.

Ben passes in the foreground with his belongings. He pauses to wave; the cotton pickers wave back.

Ben proceeds, going toward the great house that stands like a castle in the distance.

INT. HALLWAY—DAY
As Lucius and Ben climb the stairs, oak-panelled, past a great Victorian armorial window, they pause before a bedroom door. Lucius indicates the door on the right.

> LUCIUS
> Mister Jody and Miss Eula . . .
> *(on the left)*
> Miss Clara.

> BEN
> And the old man?

> LUCIUS
> Never know where he is. He don't sleep good. Moves from room to room—sometimes three in a night.

He opens the door and precedes Ben in.

INT. BEN'S BEDROOM—DAY
A large, sunny room, French doors opening to a wide veranda. Ben puts down his belongings, looks around slowly, appreciating the size.

> BEN
> I had five sisters and a brother and a father and a mother and an old lady aunt—and all together we slept in a room half this size.

> LUCIUS
> Same as my family.

> BEN
> *(smiling)*
> Well, look at us now, Lucius.

> LUCIUS
> Big rooms, small rooms—they're all the same to the Lord.

(pointing across the hall)
Bathroom over there.

He goes out. Ben bounces on the bed—he is satisfied. Having made himself at home, he strolls out.

INT. HALLWAY—DAY
He walks across the hall and throws open the bathroom door. Jody is lathering his face briskly. He turns at the interruption and his jaw drops at the sight of Ben, lounging against the doorjamb.

BEN
(easily)
Just so we won't crowd each other, I shave nights and shower mornings.

Jody stares at him. Then he grabs a towel, rubs the soap from his face with one violent gesture, and pushes past. He goes down the stairs three at a time.

EXT. DOWNSTAIRS VERANDA—DAY
Varner is at the breakfast table, eating hugely, attacking his platter hungrily. He squints up at his son as Jody comes bursting upon him.

JODY
Bringin' him *here*? Into the *house*?

Varner keeps eating, slapping butter on his toast, carving his pancakes, wolfing his food.

VARNER
Big house. We got room for one more.

JODY
He don't belong here. He's hired help!

VARNER
He's more than that.

JODY
How much more than that?

VARNER
He's goin' to be a brother to you, Jody.
(pauses)
I've brought you home a big brother. But look out. He's clever. He'll be up when you're sleepin'. He's goin' to be

where you *ain't*. So take warnin', Jody. Look alive, Jody.
You're two race horses startin' out even—we'll see who's
faster and smarter.

JODY
(intensely)
Not exactly *even*—considerin' that I'm your *blood* son.

VARNER
(harshly)
Don't open that can of beans!

JODY
I *am* openin' it!

VARNER
Then eat what you got! Exactly nothing!

JODY
Am I your son or ain't I your son?

VARNER
You was born to me.

JODY
Ain't you got any affection or regard for me? Just tell me
that.

VARNER
You tryin' to make yourself miserable?

JODY
Miserable? Seems like I walked around in misery all my
life! You ain't never been a father—except to tell me: Stand
up straight, push, reach, hurry up, stretch yourself!

VARNER
I put down a big footprint. I said: Here. Step in. Fill it.
(waves his cigar)
You never did. That made me mighty disappointed.

JODY
(trembling)
I tried! I tried to be what you wanted, but I ain't got it in
me. Where do you go lookin' for it if you ain't got it in you?

VARNER
(flat)
You find a way or you don't.

Jody makes an inarticulate attempt to talk.

VARNER
(heavily)
You have Lucius dig you up some worms, Jody, and then
you go fishin', boy . . .

Jody turns and stumbles blindly into the house.

INT. HALLWAY—DAY
*Jody goes up the stairs at a run, crashing wildly into the bannister, brushing
past Clara who is coming down. He goes slamming into his room.*

*Clara stands looking after him. Troubled, she follows. She hesitates outside
the door, then opens it gently.*

INT. JODY AND EULA'S BEDROOM—DAY
*Jody lies sprawled on the bed, his face buried in the pillows. The blinds are
drawn, the room dark.*

*Clara looks down at her brother, lying before her in defeat, silent and inert.
She sits on the edge of the bed and touches his hand.*

CLARA
Don't you lie there with your face in the pillow, Jody
Varner. That's just exactly what he expects you to be doing.
(pauses)
You had spunk once. You used to throw brown paper bags
full of water down on his head from this very window . . .
I'd fill them and you'd throw them . . .
(pauses again)
You were only seven and you were wonderful. You weren't
afraid.
(holding his hand tight)
Remember John Wesley Pritchard? He stood out in the
schoolyard one day and said, "Clara Varner has front tceth
like a horse!" And I cried and said, "I'm going to get my
brother Jody to hit you!" And you did.
(softly)
I'd never have gotten out of my girlhood alive if it hadn't

been for you. All of which makes you very dear to me,
Jody—no matter what he said or did to you downstairs . . .

*She leans over and kisses him on the cheek. His eyes glitter as he watches her
but he says nothing. She rises unhappily and goes.*

INT. BEN'S BEDROOM—NIGHT
*Ben lies smoking in bed in the dark, under a single sheet. The French doors
are thrown open to the night. He puts the cigarette out, throws back the sheet,
lies in his shorts. He is wakeful, restless, too hot to sleep. He rises suddenly,
picks up the mattress, and carries it out to the veranda.*

EXT. VERANDA—NIGHT
*He throws the mattress down, stretches out in the moonlight. Then he turns
his head and finds that he is looking through the open doors of Clara's room.*

OVER BEN'S SHOULDER—NIGHT
*Clara's reflection can be seen in her dressing mirror; she is sitting up in bed,
reading by the light of a small lamp, wearing glasses.*

                              BEN
You look pretty with reading glasses on . . .

She looks up startled, snatching the glasses off.

                              BEN
You look pretty with 'em off . . .

*Clara closes her book slowly, looks thoughtfully out to the veranda. She says
nothing.*

                              BEN
You look mighty young, Miss Clara—curled up in your
bed—like you just washed your hands and face and brushed
your teeth and said your prayers . . . like a little girl . . . I
bet you were a mighty appealing little girl. I bet your hair
hung in a tangle down your back. I bet you knew where to
find blackberries and robins' eggs. I bet you kept a doll with
no head on it.

She still says nothing.

                              BEN
There's a church bazaar coming next week. You wear a
white dress and a ribbon in your hair, and I'll waltz you
around under the moon.

She turns out her lamp. He is unable to see her any longer. There is a long silence in the soft summer darkness. Then he calls out softly, with a lilt, imitating the boys who cry after Eula:

BEN

Clara, Clara, Cla-ha-hara . . .

EXT. CHURCH BAZAAR—DAY
Strings of colored bunting ring the lawn behind the church as the population of Frenchman's Bend turn out in their summer finery for country dances and games under huge placards reading: "Church Benefit—Build a New Belfry." There are tents and booths and galvanized buckets of punch; children hot and shrieking play Pin The Tail On; three or four aged men in brushed Confederate uniforms totter weakly about on the green, evoking a day long gone by. There is a rummage sale, a kissing booth, picnic tables laden with pies and cake, a raised wooden platform shaking under a square dance—the caller's voice booms out, the fiddles clamor.

MED. SHOT—THE LOCALS—DAY
As they look after Ben thoughtfully.

BOOKWRIGHT

That Quick. Now there's a comer . . .

TULL

Name suits him. First into that farm, then into the store, then into the house—and all he started with was a book of matches.

PEABODY

He's not a *bad* fellow. But if you should go out to see him on business, go out nekkid, so you won't feel the cold comin' back.

HOUSTIN

I wish I was Ben Quick—with this here whole state of Mississippi to graze on . . .

EXT. BAZAAR—DAY
Ben wanders among the booths, nodding to an acquaintance here and there, pausing to smile at the children's games, to enjoy the square dancers. He passes the pie booth and stops when he sees Eula behind the counter.

EULA

Can I sell you somethin'? Care for a wedge of pie?

BEN

Yes, apple pie.

EULA

That'll be fifteen cents, thank you.

EXT. BY A GROVE OF TREES—DAY
*The festivity continues in the background. Minnie and Varner are some
distance away from the others.*

MINNIE

You got a pencil?

VARNER

What for?

MINNIE

I want you to write somethin' down.

VARNER

What is it?

MINNIE

September thirty. That's the day.
(pauses)
A six-layer vanilla cake is comin' from Mayville, suitably
decorated in white boiled frostin'—and a hundred and four
hand-written invitations have gone out, no children under
six years.
(nervously)
Women have to stand up for themselves—and that's what
I've done.

VARNER
(angrily)
What gall have you been up to, Minnie?

MINNIE

It's all arranged. All but the license and the blood test and
the weddin' ring—
(anxiously)
—*and* your fallin' in with it.

VARNER

I tell you what you do, Minnie. You take the six-layer cake and cut it up into a hundred and four pieces, and you send 'em out with your *regrets*!

MINNIE
(quietly)

All right, Will.

VARNER
(remorseful)

Minnie, how'd you like a bright yellow Thunderbird motor car?

MINNIE

No, thank you, Will.

VARNER

How'd you like a Singer Sewing Machine—with all the attachments?

MINNIE

No, thank you, Will.

VARNER
(heavily)

Well . . . how'd you like a plain gold band?

MINNIE
(simply)

Yes. Please, Will.

Beaming, he holds open his arms to her. She hugs him close, her eyes closed tight with gratitude.

EXT. BAZAAR—DAY
Ben finds himself in a crowd. He sees with interest that Clara is the center of a group of young ladies; Ratliff, beside her, drawls out a spiel:

RATLIFF

. . . Each of these young ladies has packed two box suppers, folks. And the high bidder wins not only the delicious vittles, but the privilege of eatin' 'em with the young lady who prepared 'em with her own delicate hands . . . Now we'll start off with the daughter of one of our first citizens—

Miss Clara Varner. How much am I offered for Miss Clara Varner's box supper?

Alan Stewart steps forward with a smile.

                    ALAN
Ten dollars.

                    RATLIFF
I'm offered ten dollars. Anybody goin' to hike that some?

Ben takes a big chew out of his pie and calls out:

                    BEN
I'll make it eleven.

                    RATLIFF
Mister Quick is interested in competin'. It's now eleven.

Clara looks at Ben swiftly. He grins at her.

                    ALAN
Twelve.

                    BEN
Thirteen.

                    ALAN
Fourteen.

                    BEN
                    (enjoying himself)
Fifteen.

                    ALAN
Sixteen.

                    CLARA
                    (low)
Alan, please!

                    BEN
Fifty.

A gasp from the crowd.

                    BEN
In a very fine cause . . .

Alan looks helplessly at Clara and shrugs. Ratliff pounds his gavel.

RATLIFF

That's the most expensive chicken supper you're ever goin'
to eat—but worth every cent of it, considerin' the company
you'll be eatin' it in.
(to Clara)
Hope you give him *de*-zert, for that price.

CLARA

He'll get his just deserts, all right.

*Ben holds up a hand to help Clara down from the platform. She thrusts a
basket with two box suppers into his hand and walks down unaided. She
moves away and Ben leisurely ambles after her.*

Ratliff leads forward the next girl, AMANDA RATLIFF.

RATLIFF

I know this young lady is a good cook 'cause I'm her daddy.
What am I offered for drum sticks and chocolate brownies?

EXT.—MOVING SHOT—BEN AND CLARA—DAY
*They walk through the crowd, she a little ahead of him. She comes to a picnic
table, throngs of people around, and turns to him.*

CLARA

Will this do?

BEN

Nope. I like my picnics in the woods.

He indicates a place in the distance with his hand. They walk on.

EXT.—BY THE RIVER BANK—DAY
*The sound of the fiddles is heard in the distance. Ben points to a spot and
Clara pauses. He takes a cloth from the basket and spreads it on the ground
with a flourish. He sits in the grass and sets out the two boxes.*

Clara stands away from him by a tree, watching him.

BEN

Come on. Either we eat it or the ants will.

She comes slowly down in the grass beside him.

CLARA

That was quite a gesture, back there. How are you going to live for the rest of the month?

BEN

I have prospects.
(opens a box)
Look what we have here. Little fancy napkins. Little frosted cakes. Little dainty sandwiches with the crusts cut off.
(smiles)
You've got a bigger appetite than this, haven't you, Miss Clara?

CLARA
(quietly)
Hog wash, Mister Quick.

BEN

Well, well.

CLARA

You heard me. Hog wash.

BEN

Strong language, Miss Clara.

CLARA

You've got some foolish ideas about me. I'm no trembling little rabbit, full of smoldering, unsatisfied desires—

BEN

Is that so?

CLARA

Yes, it's so. I'm a woman full-grown, very smart, and not at all bad to look at.

BEN

Amen.

CLARA

And I expect to live at the top of my bent, without any help from you.

BEN

You're a fire-eater, you are.

CLARA

You're barking up the wrong girl. Because it'll never be you.

A slight pause.

BEN
(grins)

Never say never.

CLARA

I don't know what arrangements you've made with my father—but you'll find you have no bargain with me.

He leans very close to her.

BEN

We're going to be married, Miss Clara. Haven't you heard?

CLARA

You've been hoodwinked, Mister Quick. For once in your life, you've been *had*.

BEN

You mean you're turning me down? Refusing my hand and my heart?

CLARA

You're too much like my father to suit me. And I'm an authority on him.

BEN
(smiling widely)

Wonderful old man.

CLARA

Yes, one wolf recognizes another.

BEN

Tame us. *You* could.

CLARA

I'm not interested. I gave up on him when I was nine years old. And I gave up on you the first minute I looked into your cold, blue eyes.

BEN
(softly)
You got the color right.

CLARA
I've got *everything* right, Mr. Quick.

BEN
Well, I can see you don't like me. But you're going to have me.
(lazily)
It'll be you and me.

CLARA
Not the longest day I live!

BEN
They'll say that's poor Clara Varner, whose father married her off to a dirt-scratching, shiftless, no-good farmer who just happened by. Well, we'll let 'em talk. I'm telling you that you'll wake up mornings *smiling*.

CLARA
(passionately)
That's not enough for me—that's not *nearly* enough! I'm a human being. Do you know what that means, Mister Quick? I set a price on myself—a high, *high* price. You may be surprised to hear it, but I've got quite a bit to give, things I've been saving up all my life—things like love and affection and understanding and jokes and good times and good cooking! I'm prepared to be the Queen of Sheba for some lucky man—or at the very least the best wife anybody could hope for!
(pauses)
That's my human history. And it's not going to be bought and sold—and it's *certainly* not going to be given away to any passing stranger.

BEN
(ferociously)
Then run! Run like hell. Buy a bus ticket and disappear. Change your name. Dye your hair. Get lost—and maybe you'll be safe from me.

> ALAN'S VOICE

Are you finished here, Clara?

WIDEN ANGLE—DAY
to include Alan standing before them. Clara rises quickly.

> CLARA

Yes, Alan, thank you. I am.

> ALAN

I'll walk you back.
> *(dryly)*

With your permission, Mister Quick.

Ben nods. Clara takes Alan's arm and they move away together.

MOVING SHOT—CLARA AND ALAN—DAY
They walk in silence a while. She laughs nervously.

> CLARA

Do I look very flustered?

> ALAN

No.

> CLARA

Well, I am. Do you mind if we stop a minute?

She stops abruptly.

MED. SHOT—CLARA AND ALAN—DAY
She leans trembling against a tree, her hands over her face. Anxiously, he comes close.

> ALAN
> *(gently)*

Is something wrong? Do you care to tell me?

> CLARA
> *(suddenly)*

Alan, this is the hardest thing I've ever had to do in my life.

> ALAN

Tell me about it and let's see if we can make it easier.

                    CLARA
                    (haltingly)
I've told people you love me. I've told *myself* you love me.
I've done that for five years . . .
                    (pauses)
But I've never heard you say it. Not once. Now I've got to
know.

                    ALAN
Then I'd better say it. I do love you, Clara.

She stares at him, divining equivocation.

                    CLARA
                    (urgently)
But do you want me—the way a man wants a woman?

                    ALAN
I want to help you.

A long pause. She shakes her head slowly.

                    CLARA
Oh, Alan. That's such a pitiful answer. Such a good, kind,
pitiful answer.

                    ALAN
It's the only kind of answer I can make you, Clara.
                    (intensely)
I didn't mean to waste your young years like this. But you
were so sweet, so graceful, so intelligent. You never made
any demands.

                    CLARA
Well, I wanted to. I came very close a couple of times.
There were all sorts of feminine wiles I was going to try out
on you. Of course, I don't suppose it would have done any
good. Your momma had a long head start on me, and I
don't think anybody's going to overtake her.

*A long pause. Clara looks brightly away from him; she tries to keep her voice
light.*

CLARA

How terrible it must have been for you. All those Friday
nights, with my dreadful father nipping at your heels—and
me, languishing and moping and dreaming over you—how
embarrassed you must have been.

(tears come to her eyes)

I'm so ashamed!

EXT.—BY RIVER BANK—DAY

Jody looks as if he is hunting, following a spoor, moving with slow concentration, his eyes gleaming, sweeping every tree and every shadow, his hair fallen disheveled into his eyes. He stops abruptly as he comes upon Ben lying under a tree, his straw hat over his eyes, fast asleep. Jody moves forward slowly. He prods the boy with his foot, bringing a pistol out of his pocket. Ben yawns and stretches, coming slowly awake; he recognizes Jody as the gun is leveled murderously at him.

BEN

(quietly)

You looking for me, Jody?

JODY

(thickly)

I'm lookin' for you and I found you!

Ben stares up into the muzzle of the gun and speaks softly.

BEN

Okay, we got that much clear. What next?

JODY

From the minute you strayed in here, everything's gone wrong
in my life! I been cut down to nothin'. I lost me my store, and
my wife's respect, and my old man hates me worse than ever.

(waves the gun wildly)

All that's over now. They'll find you downstream tomorrow, and I'll have my place back in the world!

BEN

(quietly)

If you're going to kill me, let me stand up first.

He comes slowly to his feet. Jody backs away a few steps hurriedly but the gun does not waver.

JODY

You think I'm jokin'?

Ben stands before him, thoughtful and serious.

BEN

Tell you what I'll do, Jody. I'll make it up to you. I'll pay you back for everything you think I've taken. I'll make you rich, Jody!

JODY

I don't want to hear about it!

BEN

Look.

He reaches in his pocket and pulls out a fistful of silver coins. He jingles them. Then he opens his palm. Jody looks.

JODY

So you got five dollars. Who cares?

BEN
(his eyes gleaming)

No ordinary five dollars, Jody. Not wages. Not spending money. *Treasure.*

JODY

From where?

BEN

Out of my front lawn.

A long pause.

JODY

What?

BEN
(softly)

The old Frenchman's place, Jody. You know. That your daddy gave me.

JODY

That's nothin' but a heap of bricks—an old haunted house!

BEN

That's what it appears to be . . .

JODY

Listen here. I ain't the kind to be taken in by a bunch of hokey stories old men tell while they sit around in the shade spittin' tobacco juice.

BEN

That's shrewd of you, Jody. I felt the same way myself—till idle curiosity led me to do a little poking around.

He holds out the coins reverently, his voice a whisper.

BEN

I tell you, Jody, when this turned up I was struck dumb. It's all there—just like people have said for a hundred years.

JODY
(angrily)

You tryin' to gull me!

BEN

Put your mind at ease. I know better than to try to trade you blind—especially when it's my life I'm dickering for.

JODY

It's your life all right—so *show* me.

EXT. FRENCHMAN'S PLACE—DAY

In the weed-infested garden of the old plantation. Ben sits on the ground smoking quietly while Jody digs with a fury. Jody is up to his hips in a fresh-dug trench, spading with a will; the shovel flashes; dirt is hurled aside; the soft, mealy thud of the spade in the earth is the only sound.

Jody pauses at last, wiping his brow, and turns angrily to Ben:

JODY

You and your treasure! I been diggin' an hour. Where is it?

BEN
(smiling)

It might be in the next shovelful. You can never tell.

He continues furiously. The shovel clashes and rings.

Jody's mouth falls open. He looks at Ben wide-eyed. Then he bends to grapple with something in a panting frenzy—triumphantly he lifts a heavy solid sack of ancient, moldering cloth. Coins spill out of the sack, silver dollars pour out and lie gleaming.

The two young men stand staring at each other, almost in awe.

EXT. FRENCHMAN'S PLACE—NIGHT—LATER
Jody is alone, up to his waist in another fresh-dug trench, his shovel flying, hurling the dirt over his shoulder. The coins still lie spilled out on the ground. He works by the light of a lantern.

Varner comes slowly across the lawn to him. He stands a long moment, frowning down at his son.

> VARNER

Jody.

Jody whirls and stares up at his father, the shovel arrested in midair.

> VARNER

Another five minutes and the whole county'll be here, watchin' you go off your mind.

> JODY
> *(quietly)*

Get away from me.

> VARNER

Your wife is worried about you, boy. Now you climb out of that hole and come along with me.

> JODY

I said, get away.

> VARNER

I ain't goin' without you, Jody.

Jody suddenly throws back his head and laughs. His body shakes uncontrollably, he roars with laughter.

> JODY

Go on! Go on! Keep on thinkin' I'm crazy! I'm about as crazy as a fox!
> *(joyfully)*
I'm out from under your thumb, Papa! I paid that Ben Quick friend of yours one thousand dollars for the rights to this land—and everything I find here is mine!
> *(laughs again)*
I may be openin' a store right across the street from yours—who knows!

VARNER
(troubled)
Jody, what do you think you're goin' to find down in that pit?

Jody points gleefully to the pile of dollars.

JODY
More of that! Buckets of that!

VARNER
(quietly)
You've been had by that fellow Quick.

JODY
Have I! Pick it up! Bite on it! It's real, all right!

Varner picks up one of the coins. He studies it grimly.

VARNER
Is this the money that was hidden away when folks heard Grant was comin'? Is this the money that's been layin' here lost since the days of the War Between the States?

JODY
Yes!

VARNER
Look at it again. Look at it, financier! These pieces are minted in Philadelphia in 1910.
(angrily)
Ben Quick salted this place. It only cost him twenty-five silver dollars, buried out here one night in a canvas bag, to catch a sucker like you.

With a roar of pain Jody flings his shovel away. He scrambles out of the trench, fresh dirt on his hands and on his face; like one maddened he throws himself upon his father and wrenches the coin out of his hand. Gasping, hysterical, he examines the coin, holding it close to his squinting eyes. Then with a cry he throws it away. He goes to his knees and paws through the pile of dollars, picking up one after another to look at it, to read the date—each of them is flung away with another panting cry.

He turns and walks away. Jody sits slowly, sits dazed and empty on the ground.

EXT. VARNER HOUSE—DAWN
The sky is rosy with light as Clara comes back to her house and pulls in beside her father's jeep in the drive. She turns off the ignition and sits a moment behind the wheel, abstracted, lost, exhausted. Wearily, she gets out of the car.

WIDEN ANGLE—DAWN
Varner emerges on the veranda, wrapped in his red bathrobe. He leans on the rail and calls to her.

> VARNER
> Come have a nightcap with me, Sister.

INT. VARNER'S STUDY—DAWN
as Clara follows Varner into the room.

> VARNER
> Everything's settled with Alan?

> CLARA
> *(slowly)*
> Yes. It's all settled . . .

A wide smile breaks on his face.

> VARNER
> Do you mean that?
> *(she nods)*
> I'm gonna drink to that.
> *(he does)*
> I thought Ben might be the one. I would have laid odds. But Stewart is more your dish. Well, so be it. Stewart it is. Good name, good family, a little weak—but we'll bolster him up.

> CLARA
> I'm very tired now, Papa. I'd like to go to bed.

> VARNER
> *(gently)*
> No. Stay. Talk a little. This is a night for a father and daughter to talk.

> CLARA
> Finally?

VARNER

I know, I know. There's been a long, bad silence between us. But now's a time for openin' our hearts.
(wryly)
I got one, you know.

CLARA

Have you, Papa?

VARNER

I can tell you. I've eaten the bread of sorrow. I've gone around with bitterness chokin' me. Parents and children! I've asked myself what are children for? Why does a man have 'em?
(triumphantly)
Now I know! Tonight I know!

CLARA

Do you?

He is suddenly contrite; it makes him tender.

VARNER

I been hard on you. But don't feel pushed. You're goin' in the right direction. A woman's only half a thing without a man.

CLARA
(dully)
What do you know about women, Papa?

VARNER
(an outcry)
I had the best! Your mother and I were as close as two people ever get to each other. I wanted to be with that woman all the time—look at her, listen to her, touch her— she lit up the whole world for me!
(exultantly)
And I'll tell you something remarkable. That woman loved me!

There is pathos in his sudden appeal, his desire to be believed.

VARNER

She did, Clara! Can you believe that about me? A fat, ugly old redneck like me? . . .

                         CLARA
                         (numbly)
You were lucky, Papa . . .

                         VARNER
You'll be lucky too. We were born under a star, you and me.

                         CLARA
You and me . . .

                         VARNER
                         (with a sudden qualm)
Tell me something, baby. And look at me. Did I do wrong?
I mean—imposin' my will on you. Shovin' you this way and
that.
                         (softly)
Sometimes the strong go rollin' right over the weak.

                         CLARA
                         (quietly)
Sometimes . . .

EXT. STEWART HOUSE—DAY
*Mrs. Stewart is out front cutting roses as the jeep pulls up and Will Varner
heaves himself out. He strides up the walk toward her with a beaming smile.*

                    MRS. STEWART
Good mornin', Will Varner. What brings you?

*Without replying, he puts his arms around her in a bear hug, picks her up
and swings her around with elation. She squeals in outrage.*

                    MRS. STEWART
What's come over you, you old fool!

                         VARNER
Don't you give it a thought, Elizabeth. It's all in the family
now.

EXT. STEWART GARDEN—DAY
as Varner approaches Alan, who is finishing his breakfast.

                         VARNER
Pour me a cup of coffee, Alan.

He does.

VARNER

Bygones are bygones, son. You come with me. I'll show
you what's goin' to be yours. There's a substantial dowry
goes with this girl. It'll take us most of the day to look at it,
but we're makin' an early start.

ALAN

Dowry?

VARNER

You don't think I'd send Clara to you without a stitch, do
you? I take care of my own. And I'm givin' you the means
to take care of her.

ALAN
(slowly)
Mister Varner, you're making a mistake.

The words stop Varner cold. He stares at Alan.

VARNER

You mean there's no engagement between you two?

ALAN

None at all.

*Varner reacts, white with anger. He slams his fist down on the Stewarts'
garden table, shattering glassware and china with the force of his blow.*

VARNER
(a bellow of outrage)
That girl lied to me!

MRS. STEWART

Have you lost your mind, Will Varner?

VARNER

Madam, shut up! I'm talkin' to your son!

ALAN

If you'll quiet down, I'll tell you something. I'm no good for
your daughter. I never was. I never could be . . .

MRS. STEWART

My boy doesn't need any traffic with your family, Will
Varner. He never wanted it. Your girl pushed it on him.

ALAN
(angrily)
Mother, that isn't true! Keep out of this!

VARNER
(to Alan)
You keep your mouth shut about this. I don't want this community to know my daughter's been jilted by anybody like you.

MRS. STEWART
We're not given to gossip around here.

VARNER
Keep a tight lip! You breathe a word of this and I'll come after you with my bare hands!

He wheels around and goes. Mrs. Stewart looks at her son complacently.

MRS. STEWART
You goin' to be home all day, sonny?

ALAN
(defeated)
I'll be home . . .

EXT. MOVING SHOT—VARNER—DAY
as Varner drives home in his jeep. The vehicle is like a weapon in his angry hands. A truck labors ahead of him. He passes, cuts back too sharply—to avoid collision the truck driver goes off the road into a ditch, and sits there, cursing hotly. Varner races on grimly, unaware of the damage.

EXT. STORE—DAY
Varner turns into the street on two wheels. He careens to a stop in the middle of the road and leans on his horn. Ben steps out on the gallery in response to the shrill summons. Varner shouts at him from the middle of the street:

VARNER
You got a blue suit—get it cleaned! You got a pair of shoes—get 'em shined! Get a haircut! You're goin' to be married!

The jeep churns away. Ben looks after it quizzically.

INT. SCHOOL—DAY
Clara is seated at her desk.

Varner comes striding into the back of the room. Clara's eyes widen at the sight of him. He shouts at her.

> **VARNER**
> You'll find him at the store! Get yourself down there! Now! Just say one word: Yes!

He goes; the door slams behind him.

EXT. VARNER HOUSE—DAY
Lucius meets Varner in front of the house as he returns.

> **LUCIUS**
> The mare has foaled, Mister Varner. Happened about half an hour ago. He's a real beauty . . .

> **VARNER**
> *(nodding)*
> I'll have a look.

He walks off toward the barn.

INT. BARN—DAY
Varner enters, leaving the door open behind him. He comes forward in the gloom to a bed of straw, where the new foal lies wet and weak. Varner kneels beside the animal and strokes its head softly.

> **VARNER**
> I'm glad *somethin'* around here is gettin' born . . .

He takes a cloth and begins wiping the foal off carefully. Its head lies in his lap. He cleans the flanks gently.

The barn is suddenly dark as the door slams shut, is bolted and locked. A horse whinnies in alarm. Even the foal seems alerted to danger, struggling weakly in Varner's arms. The old man looks toward the locked door.

> **VARNER**
> Jody? . . .

There is no answer from without. The afternoon is very still.

> **VARNER**
> Jody . . . I know it's you out there . . .

Still no reply. Varner's voice is quite even.

VARNER
Jody, at least let the horses out . . .

It is very still outside. Varner cradles the foal in his arms, stroking it.

EXT. BARN—DAY
Jody holds a flaming rag in his hand. He calls out hoarsely:

JODY
I said I'd do it! I warned you! I gave you notice.

He shuts his eyes and grits his teeth and with a savage gesture throws the burning torch onto the roof of the barn.

A horse whinnies in fear from within. Jody backs away in horror. He turns to run.

But he stops. He comes back. He stands as though mesmerized, his breath rattling in his throat. His hands clench and unclench. He turns again to run, but smoke rising from the dried-out old roof stops him once more.

The old barn catches fire quickly. Smoke begins to pour, turns black and greasy, makes an ugly wreath in the summer sky. Now the walls burst into flame with a crackle. Jody watches with his mouth open and tears inexplicably streaming from his eyes.

JODY
I'm not sorry! I'm not sorry! I'm not sorry!

The entire barn is now in roaring flame. Jody screams.

JODY
Papa!

He rushes forward, his thick fingers fumbling with the lock. It will not open. Moaning and weeping he rips it off its rusted hinges, throws open the door. Smoke bellows out into his face, the horses clatter out with shrill cries to safety. He puts an arm over his face and ducks inside.

He emerges in a moment with his father in his arms and puts him down in the grass. He turns and goes back into the inferno and comes out again with the foal.

Varner lies coughing weakly on the ground. Jody's face is black, singed; his shirt gives off wisps of smoke. He claps himself violently, rips the shirt off his back.

Then he kneels to look passionately at his father, his face ugly with grime and tears.

> JODY

Are you hurt any! Are you all right!

Varner smiles up at him.

> VARNER

You got hell fire and damnation in you, Jody Varner—
> *(puts up a trembling hand and touches his son's cheek)*
But you also got redemption . . .

> JODY
> *(shaking violently)*

Papa! . . .

> VARNER

Lord, when I think of the hate that put me in that barn and locked the door and set fire to it—
> *(his eyes shining)*
And when I think of the love that wouldn't let me go—that dragged me out again!
> *(taking Jody by the shoulders)*
I got me a son again. I got me a good right hand and a left.

EXT. THE SQUARE—DAY
The whole town has turned out to stare at the geyser of black smoke in the distance. Some grab buckets and begin to run. Others mill about angrily in what is quickly becoming a mob.

EXT. STORE—DAY
Ben comes out on the gallery of the store to look grimly at the flames. HOMER LENTZ, Jody's sycophant, shouts at him from among the press of men.

> HOMER

There's just one man in town settles his accounts with fire!

Ben looks at Homer thoughtfully. Wilk holds up a coil of hemp.

> WILK

Remember this rope? I was supposed to catch me a horse with this rope, a horse I never seen since. Maybe I can find another use for it now . . .

Ben looks calmly at Ratliff on the gallery.

> BEN
>
> This is the story of my life. Why doesn't anybody ever want to consult with me peaceable?

> RATLIFF
> *(quietly)*
>
> I wouldn't fool with them folks. I'd light out.

> BEN
> *(stubbornly)*
>
> I'm just not in a running mood.

The crowd moves sullenly toward the gallery and Ben. But Clara's Cadillac darts in swiftly to the foot of the steps, between Ben and the mob.

> CLARA
> *(urgently)*
>
> Get in!

> BEN
> *(mocking)*
>
> What's it to you if I do or I don't, Miss Clara?

> CLARA
>
> Get in!

He looks at her white face; he looks at the crowd. Then he gets quickly into the car.

Clara blasts her horn and guns the motor. The people surround them. She inches forward, nudging the closest with her bumper. For a moment no one gives way, angry faces look in on them. She blasts again; a few in front part; she takes the narrow opening and races through it. Bitter, hostile faces look after them.

EXT. BACK OF THE VARNER HOUSE—DAY
Clara pulls in and turns off the ignition. Through the gate of the back garden, through the masses of honeysuckle and Cherokee roses, they can see, without being seen, the long line of volunteer fire fighters and their hoses and buckets. The fire is out, the barn now a charred, jagged skeleton.

> BEN
>
> I'm sick of that sight!

She turns in the seat to look at him. His voice is suddenly thin with a fury of passion.

BEN

I've seen fifty fires like that. Maybe a hundred. I've watched men with their shirts ablaze. I've seen horses cook. I grew up with the smell of gasoline around me, kerosene, coal oil, anything that would burn. My old man kept 'em in case he had a grudge he wanted to settle. My old man. My father.
(he pauses; then in a monotone)
The last time I saw him I was ten years old, lying in a ditch, crying my eyes out, praying that God would strike me dead. That was the night I'd run ahead to tell on him, to turn him in, to warn a farmer that he was coming with his torch. I remember choking on my own tears, and I remember a house burning, and I remember men on horseback and the sound of shots and my father running . . .
(sits beside her quietly a while)
Maybe those shots killed him. Maybe he died in one of the fires he set. I don't know. I never saw him again.

CLARA
(moved)
That must have been terrible . . .

BEN

The terrible part came later. Knocking around the country-side. Floating around from town to town. Looking in on other people's kitchen windows from the outside . . . Boy, that man sure left his mark on me. I've got his name. And I can't run away from that.

CLARA

Yes, you can! People are kinder than you think!

BEN

Well, I wouldn't give 'em that satisfaction. I wouldn't tell 'em anything, anytime.

CLARA

Then change your name! Get rid of it!

He smiles slightly at this sympathetic outburst from her.

                    BEN
I'm a proud man, Miss Clara. The name is Quick. No
matter how much people hate it.

                    CLARA
                (slowly)
I was one of them. I hated it . . .

                    BEN
No, ma'am. You hated *me*.

                    CLARA
I guess I did.

                    BEN
                (softly)
You're a hard-headed, soft-hearted woman, Miss Clara. I
like you a whole lot.

                    CLARA
                (slowly)
You do, do you?

                    BEN
Yes, ma'am.
                (thoughtfully)
I do. All of a sudden I do.

He looks at her a long moment and then releases her.

                    BEN
                (quietly)
If you can try to save my life, Miss Clara, then I guess I can
return the favor. I can let you go.

She stares at him. He smiles.

                    BEN
Nothing to it. Pack my two straw suitcases, say goodbye to
millions. I won't even start feeling sorry I did it till I'm a
mile and a half out of Frenchman's Bend.

He gets out of the car abruptly. He lingers another moment.

                    BEN
Well, you couldn't tame me. But you taught me.

He turns around and goes cheerfully toward the house.

EXT. FRONT OF VARNER'S HOUSE—DAY
The fire fighters come streaming onto the front lawn, faces black with char, carrying their hoses and buckets as a group of men from town approach Ben menacingly. Varner turns to them and bellows:

VARNER
Now, hold on there! Wait a minute!

WILK
What about Ben Quick? We can't let that fire bug get away with it.

VARNER
The fire's out—

(indicates the fire fighters)
—thanks to you all.

ARMISTEAD
But who started it?

VARNER
It was done by an old jackass name of Varner. Dropped my cigar in the hay. Ain't that right, Jody?

JODY
That's right, Papa.

WILK
I guess our job's done, then.

VARNER
Now you all come out here on Sunday, and we'll open some kegs of beer and have us a party.

Minnie Littlejohn suddenly pushes through the crowd and runs up the steps into Varner's arms.

MINNIE
(breathlessly)
Will, Will, are you all right? I heard you was in that barn!

VARNER
In and out. Simmer down. You ain't a rich widow yet.

She hugs him gratefully.

EXT. VARNER HOUSE—DAY
as they all head for the front door.

> BEN
> If you've got a minute, Will, I'll be saying good-bye.

> VARNER
> You goin' somewhere?

> BEN
> Yeah, I'm leaving. Soon as I get my things together.

> VARNER
> What's the matter? Don't the room and board suit you here?

> BEN
> *(genially)*
> No complaints about that.

> VARNER
> Well?

> BEN
> Will, you and me have been in business only a little while. Just one hot summer. We started out playing a horseflesh game. Remember?

> VARNER
> Get to the point!

> BEN
> Point is: now we've left horses and gotten around to people. That's something else again . . .

> VARNER
> What people are you talkin' about?

Ben looks at Clara with a smile.

> BEN
> Clara—daughter to Will Varner—

> VARNER
> *(to Clara, abruptly)*
> You want to stay and hear this?

CLARA
(quietly)
Papa, wild horses wouldn't drag me off this porch.

VARNER
(glaring at Ben again)
You got my interest! You got my attention!

BEN
Will, in all this scheming we've done, we've forgotten about folks, you and me.

VARNER
I get preached to on Sundays!

BEN
(going on gently)
Yeah, but you don't listen. And neither have I, up to now . . . I didn't take easy to the idea—in fact, I've been a little slow coming around to it—but life's a valuable thing, to be treated with some respect.
(he grins)
You're old enough to know that, and I'm young enough to learn it.

CLARA
(quietly)
Isn't that the truth?

Ben puts out his hand to the old man.

BEN
So I'll be seeing you around, Will.

Varner slaps his hand aside and bellows:

VARNER
First of all, bucko, I ain't given you permission to call me by my front name!

Minnie puts a restraining hand on Varner.

MINNIE
Will, that shoutin' ain't becomin' to you . . .

He pulls away from her.

VARNER

And second of all, don't tell *me* what life is like. Life around here is what I *say* it is.

BEN

You can't have it your way, Will.

VARNER

I got influence! I'll dog you wherever you go! I'll *break* you!

BEN
(with affection)
No, you won't. You'll miss me.

Ben goes into the house.

VARNER
(addressing Clara)
What are you grinnin' about?

Clara goes into the house, giggling. Varner turns to Minnie.

VARNER

There's your gratitude. There's your thanks. I put that boy where there was fast, easy money just laying there. I put him in the Garden of Eden and let him dip his bread in honey. And he's got the all-out gall to tell me no!

INT. BEN'S ROOM—EVENING
Ben is packing his bag as Clara speaks.

CLARA

So you run . . . and you keep on running . . . and you buy yourself a bus ticket . . . and you disappear . . . and you change your name and dye your hair . . . and maybe, just maybe, you might be safe from me . . .

The speech is her declaration. They draw into a passionate embrace.

INT. VARNER ENTRY HALL—EVENING
Varner hears Ben and Clara laughing upstairs. He turns to Minnie and takes her into his arms.

VARNER

Don't I know human nature? Didn't I say that fellow Quick was meant for my Clara? I'm gonna be a grandfather. I am, Minnie.

(laughs)
It sure is good to be alive on a summer evening. Alive with friends and family and a big, healthy woman to love you.
(with emphasis)
I like life, Minnie! I like it so much I might just live forever!

THE END

Hud

Produced by Martin Ritt and Irving Ravetch, *Hud* was released by Paramount Pictures in 1963. Its cast included:

Hud Bannon .... Paul Newman
Homer Bannon .... Melvyn Douglas
Alma .... Patricia Neal
Lon Bannon .... Brandon deWilde
Burris .... Whit Bissell
Jesse .... Crahan Denton
Jose... Val Avery
Thompson .... Sheldon Allman
Larker .... Pitt Herbert
George .... Peter Brooks
Truman Peters................................. Curt Conway
Lily Peters .... Yvette Vickers
Joe Scanlon................................... George Petrie
Hermy .... John Ashley

FADE IN:

EXT. FULL PANORAMIC VISTA—DAY
The plains of Texas. Green, brown, and gray, they are spread wide under a clear sky already beginning to shimmer with early morning heat. It is a vast, lonely land, dwarfing animal and man.

The highway cuts straight through the bright, unshaded, open country, a powder-dry road pointing north to Amarillo and Raton, south to Dallas, Houston, or Fort Worth. The dawn is just ending, the sun starting its long climb.

The sound of "The Wabash Cannonball" BLARES out over the prairie. It is an Ernest Tubb recording, unlikely Western jazz for this early in the day, an incongruous background for serene and empty space.

EXT. THALIA
The gold rays of the sun flash on the chrome of an old truck as it slows down to enter town. Thalia, Texas, is one of those unseen little places along the highway where some roads end and others begin. It is a sun-parched oasis, a town of unpainted houses and grassless yards full of pea vines, goatheads, and weeds.

EXT. MAIN STREET
LON BANNON swings his long legs out of the truck. He is seventeen, a guileless, courteous boy hovering between the daydreams of youth and the realities of maturity. He leans back in to speak to HANK HUTCH, the driver.

LON

Thanks for the lift.

107

HANK

Where you gonna look for him?

LON
(shrugging)

I don't know. If I find a pink Cadillac, he'll be around somewhere.

He waves to the man and the truck grinds up the street, the only moving thing in Thalia at this hour. Lon swings across the road and pokes his head into the all-night truckers' café.

INT. CAFÉ

The place is empty as Lon enters. It turns out that Tubb's wailing voice is coming from the boy's shirt front; like a lot of teenagers he is a slave to the transister radio and carries one in his pocket at all times. Right now he reaches in and turns the VOLUME way down.

DAISY'S VOICE hails him from a room at the rear.

DAISY'S VOICE

Who's that?

LON

Lon.

DAISY'S VOICE

Oh, hi, Lonnie. I'm back here makin' chili. You want breakfast, I'll come out.

LON

No, thanks. Daisy, you seen my Uncle Hud?

DAISY'S VOICE

I chicken-fried him a steak last night around seven o'clock. I haven't seen him since.

LON

All right.
(opens the pie case)
I'm takin' two doughnuts, Daisy.

DAISY'S VOICE

Okay, honey. Leave a dime on the register.

Lon puts down a coin and goes out, cramming doughnut into his mouth.

EXT. MAIN STREET
The boy comes out wiping powdered sugar down the side of his jeans. MISTER SKAAGS, wearing an apron and a frown, is standing in front of "Skaags Bar and Grill," stretching brown tape over what remains of a broken plate glass window.

LON
You musta had quite a brawl in here last night.

SKAAGS
(sourly)
I had *Hud* in here last night is what I had.

LON
(sympathetically)
Sure looks it.

The boy recrosses the road, looking both ways for some sign of his uncle. He ambles around a corner.

EXT. SIDE STREET
LARKER, one of the locals, is up on a ladder, stringing a canvas sign across the road, which announces the coming of the annual rodeo. The man greets Lon as he appears.

LARKER
Hey, there, Lon.

LON
How are you, Mister Larker?

LARKER
You gonna rodeo this year, Lon?

LON
(shakes his head)
Not me. I'm not lookin' to get my stomach stepped on.

LARKER
What're you doin' in town this early?

LON
Tryin' to run down Hud.

LARKER
Hud? Didn't I see that big Cadillac car of his parked right around the corner? Pretty sure I did.

Lon nods and starts away. Larker calls after him warningly.

> LARKER
>
> I don't know if I'd go disturbin' him, if I was you.

> LON
> *(uneasy enough as it is)*
> Well, I'm not dying to. But I've been told to get him.

He goes down the street and turns another corner.

EXT. SCANLON HOUSE

The car he is looking for is parked at the curb in front of a quiet, shuttered house. Directly in the middle of the path leading to the door is a woman's high-heeled shoe. Lon picks it up and turns it around in his hands thoughtfully. Then he goes up on the porch and puts the shoe down very gently. He raises a fist to knock—but thinks better of it. He backs away uncertainly, off the porch and down the path again. While mulling over what to do he reaches in and turns the radio OFF completely.

Finally he calls out tentatively.

> LON

Hud?

The street is very still. He gets louder.

> LON

Hud!

He waits a while and then with sudden resolution leans inside the car and HITS the HORN.

This brings results at last. Hud comes out, stuffing his shirt-tail into his pants.

HUD BANNON is in his thirties. He is an easy, careless man, with eyes that have the disconcerting trick of remaining too steadily on people and objects. There is no suggestion at the moment that his nerves can tighten like wire around a hay bale, that he trusts nobody. When Hud is interested and cares to be, he is as good as the best and more reckless than the wildest of the thousand wild-ass cowboys in the Texas cattle country.

> HUD
> *(evenly)*
> Honcho, I hope for your sake that this house is on fire.

LON

I'm sorry to roust you out, but we got some trouble at the ranch.

HUD

Bub, you got trouble right here. I was just gettin' nicely tucked in, when you come tiptoeing through the tulips.

LON
(doggedly)
Granddad wants you. He said right now.

HUD

He said right now, did he?
(with easy sarcasm)
You think maybe it would be all right with my old daddy if I stopped to button up my shirt?

LON

Come on, willya, Hud?

HUD

You got me out of the wrong side of the bed this morning. So don't snap at my heels. I'm liable to turn around and bite you.

Hud takes out a pocket comb and begins to comb his tousled head, moving toward the car. At that moment an old Buick turns into the driveway and stops. JOE SCANLON gets out, pulling a heavy suitcase with him. He stares in disbelief at the two men, his face hardening suspiciously.

SCANLON

Which one of you two is comin' out of my house at six o'clock in the morning?

HUD
(pleasantly)
Joe, how are you?

SCANLON

I asked you a question! Which *one*, dammit!

HUD

I hate to have to tell you, seein' as how it's my own nephew, but it's this snot-nosed kid here.

> *(Lon pales)*

I been lookin' for him all night. Just flushed him out a couple of minutes ago.

                    SCANLON
I'll kill the little punk!

                    HUD
                    (barring his way)
Simmer down, Joe—

                    SCANLON
Get out of my way, Hud!

                    LON
                    (desperately)
Wait a minute, Mister Scanlon—

                    SCANLON
Just lemme at that kid—

Scanlon, his fists doubled, bumps against Hud in his eagerness to get at Lon, who has ducked defensively behind his uncle.

                    HUD
Now, Joe, you know you got sugar diabetes. You just take it easy. I'll handle this thing for you.

                    SCANLON
I don't *need* any help from you. I'll do it myself!

                    HUD
You can't afford to let yourself get worked up like that, old buddy. I'll lower his temperature some, I promise you.
                    (to Lon, still shielding him)
Come on, hotrod! *Move.* You and I are gonna finish this little discussion in the woodshed!

He shoves Lon roughly into the car. Scanlon stands fuming on the pavement as Hud guns the Cadillac and LURCHES away from the house.

INT. CAR—MOVING SHOT
Hud smiles to himself as he wheels the car onto the highway and heads for home. Lon is indignant.

                    LON
Thanks! Thanks a whole lot!

HUD

Relax. You're gonna be able to charge a stud fee by the time this story gets around town.

LON

If I'm still alive. I coulda got hurt back there, you know that?

HUD

So could I.
(he grins)
Ain't it lucky you were handy?

The boy smiles ruefully at last. He sues for the friendship he longs to have from this man.

LON

Maybe you ought to take me along as a regular thing.

HUD
(shakes his head)
The pace would kill you, sonny.

Hud feeds the gas and the car leaps ahead on the empty road.

HUD

Now that the dust has settled, what's so red-hot important that my daddy has to drag me back on my day off?

LON

He wants to ask your advice about something.

Mention of the old man seems to darken Hud's mood.

HUD

Ask *me*? He hasn't asked me about anything in fifteen years. I just work out there from the shoulders down, myself.

LON
(uneasily)
Well, don't get sore about it.
(a slight silence)
You gonna be able to make it all day, after a night like you put in?

> HUD

I ain't a hundred years old, like him. I don't need a week of
sleep to be fresh.

> LON
> *(quietly)*

He can't help being an old man, Hud.

EXT. THE HIGHWAY—FULL SHOT
*The pink Cadillac chews up the road, hurtling to the horizon. Far up ahead it
turns suddenly, glinting in the sun, and speeds the final stretch to the Bannon
house.*

EXT. BANNON HOUSE
*as the car roars in. Hud hits the brakes and burns gravel right up to the shade
trees in the front yard.*

INT. KITCHEN BANNON HOUSE
*HOMER BANNON, Lon's Granddad, Hud's father, puts down his coffee
cup. He addresses ALMA, housekeeper and cook.*

> GRANDDAD

That'll be Hud.

> ALMA

He's parked right in my flower bed.

*Homer is in his eighties, the sandy hair of his head still thick as ever. He is
one of the last of his breed, a man of simplicity, ethics, and iron obligation.*

*Alma Brown is a tall woman, shapely, comfortable, and pretty. She has an indul-
gent knowledge of the world, and it makes for a flat, humorous, candid manner.
At the moment she is mixing batter near the sink, a cigarette in her mouth.*

*Hud and Lon enter. There is always tension when Hud and Granddad face
each other, though the old man's attitude is almost invariably polite and mild.*

> GRANDDAD

Good mornin', Hud. Close the screen door, Lonnie—we're
gettin' a lot of flies in here.

> HUD
> *(sarcastic)*

Well, I see the house is still standin'. And you're pourin'
coffee in your saucer, same as usual. How come you pushed
the panic button on me?

GRANDDAD

I was sorry to cut into your time off, but we come up with a
dead heifer in the night. I'm kinda curious about what killed
her.

HUD

Was she cut or crippled looking? Any swelling on her?
Could have been a snake bite.

GRANDDAD

Nothing like that at all. That's what kinda worries me. This
may be something I need to know about. Jesse and Jose are
out there now keepin' off the buzzards.

ALMA
(abruptly)

Stay out of those berries, Lon. They're going in the pie.

Lon has absently put his hand in a bowl of fruit; he withdraws it hastily.

HUD

Well, let's not stand around here till dinner. I got other
things to do today.
(to Alma)
Watch that cigarette ash. It's going in the pot.

GRANDDAD
(rising)

I'll go bring the pickup around.

*The old man walks out. Lon hesitates a moment and then follows him. Hud
pours himself coffee and gulps it hurriedly.*

ALMA

How come you're always running your car over my zinnias?
I've been trying to get those things to come up for two weeks.

HUD

Don't plant 'em where I park.

ALMA

You're cheerful this morning.

HUD
(irritably)

Missy, your job is to keep house, not to worry about my
disposition.

ALMA

Pan's still on. Want a couple of fried eggs? Or did you have breakfast in bed?

HUD
(dryly)
No, we hadn't quite gotten around to breakfast.

Hud puts his cup in the sink and goes out.

EXT. PASTURE
The truck stops and the three men get out. JESSE and JOSE, the two cowhands, have been sitting beside the carcass. They rise as Granddad greets them.

GRANDDAD

Good mornin', boys.

JESSE

Mister Bannon . . .
(points to the buzzards)
Hard to keep them birds off. Had to use a flashlight most of the night.

There are about fifty in the trees around, nodding their scabby bald heads and raising their wings. A few, more bold, waddle cautiously toward the heifer.

Hud suddenly drags a rifle out of the truck and begins to SHOOT, working the pump-action as fast as he can, six or eight shots before he runs out of bullets. Three of the buzzards are dead, the rest rise from the limbs of the trees like springboard divers.

HUD
(disgusted)
Look at those buzzards. You couldn't keep 'em scared off with artillery.

GRANDDAD
(mildly)
Wish you wouldn't do that. They keep the country clean. Besides, there's a law against killin' buzzards.

HUD
I always say the law was meant to be interpreted in a lenient manner. That's what I try to do myself. Sometimes I lean to one side of it, sometimes I lean to the other.

GRANDDAD
(gently)
I don't like to break the law on my place, Hud.

Hud gives him a strange grin. Then all five of them squat down around the carcass, studying it in silence.

HUD
Well, she's not gonna sit up and tell us herself.

GRANDDAD
What do you think, Hud?

HUD
I don't know the answer. She looks clean to me.

GRANDDAD
Something killed her. I think I'll call up the state vet. He might know.

HUD
What for? This is our land. I don't want any government men on it anytime, anyplace, anywhere. This ain't nothing. Just leave her lay and let the buzzards have her.

The two men's eyes meet. Granddad speaks softly as always.

GRANDDAD
Oh, I don't believe I will.
(slight pause)
Before I go to bed, I'll call the government man and ask him to come out and take a look at it.

HUD
That's the stuff. Bring in some jelly bean to tell you how to run your own business. But don't bother askin' me what I think from now on.

GRANDDAD
I'd like for you and Lon to stay out here a while. I'll take these boys back with me so they can snooze a little.
(hands Hud a metal can out of the truck)
You take this water can, so you won't parch.

Jesse and Jose climb in with Granddad and the three men drive back across the pasture, leaving Hud and Lon alone. The boy watches his uncle gravely.

                              HUD
You can sit up with our sick friend here. I got a healthy one
in town that won't wait.

He yanks the boy's Stetson down over his ears and starts blithely away.

*Lon pushes his hat back, reaches in idly to turn on his transistor. The
SOUND of "Driftwood on the River" TRUMPETS out. The boy sits hugging his knees beside the dead heifer, listening to the music, an isolated figure
in the big pasture.*

EXT. THALIA—DAY
*The pickup truck from the ranch is broken down at the curb with a flat tire.
Jesse is in the background, wrestling a wheel off. Alma is half-seated on a
fender, chin in her hand, two large bags of groceries piled in her lap. She
catches sight of Hud's car and jumps up to wave at him.*

                             ALMA
Hey! Hey, stop, will you!

EXT. HUD'S CAR
Hud pulls up. Alma hoists the heavy bags and staggers over to him.

                             ALMA
It's a good thing you showed up. We blew a tire on the
pickup, and I gotta get this stuff back for dinner.

*Meanwhile she is trying to get the door open, balancing one of the bags on
her knee. Hud sits unconcerned behind the wheel.*

                             ALMA
You think your hand'd fall off if you opened the door?

He clamly pushes the door open for her, but makes no attempt to help.

INT. HUD'S CAR
as Alma falls into the front seat beside him in a welter of groceries.

*Hud starts up again and heads for the highway, while she rearranges her
things and settles back.*

                              HUD
Did you pick up my beer?

                             ALMA
Two six-packs. That ought to see you till tomorrow.

                    HUD
You keepin' count on me?

                    ALMA
I'm always trippin' over those empties, I know that.

He looks at her coolly. They drive in silence a while. Her nose twitches.

                    ALMA
Boy, somebody in this car smells of Chanel Number Five. It
isn't me—I can't afford it.
                    (an amused, sidelong glance)
You sure weren't riding the range this afternoon, were you?

                    HUD
You bein' smart?

                    ALMA
No. I just wish I knew where some gals get the time during
the day.
                    (shakes her head)
I don't know. By the time I get through scrubbing that kitchen
floor, cleaning the bathtub, and hanging out the wash . . .

                    HUD
They just drop everything, honey.

                    ALMA
                    (shrugs)
Well, I suppose it does beat housework.

She reaches into one of the bags.

                    ALMA
Want an orange? Peel it for you.
                    (starts peeling one)
Look at that. Says "Florida" on it. We grow 'em right here
in Texas and they send 'em all the way in from Florida.
That makes sense, doesn't it?

*She breaks off a segment of orange, pops it into her mouth. She speaks with
a mouth full.*

                    ALMA
                    (casually)
The checker in the A&P market says it's Truman Peters's
wife you're seeing.

HUD

Is that what he says?

ALMA

He says she's got a bad temper. He says her maid quit her cause she hollers so much.

HUD

Well, *our* maid's gonna get canned for talkin' too much.

She shrugs again, dips in the bag, rips open a Nabisco package.

ALMA

You want a fig newton?

HUD

Leave somethin' there for dinner, will you?

She puts the package back wryly, looking at him, still amused. He watches the road, speeding for home.

INT. KITCHEN—BANNON HOUSE—NIGHT
The kitchen is steamy, windows open wide, bull bats swooping toward the light and striking against the screen. Alma has served Lon and Granddad dinner, slouching through the meal with easy grace in her runover bedroom slippers. The boy swirls his last hunk of bread in the last drops of gravy on his plate.

ALMA

I don't believe it. You're still eating bread? After I gave you steak and flour gravy and hominy, and fried okra and onions and hot rolls?

LON
(grins)
It looked like a lot when we sat down, but it sure melted away.

GRANDDAD

Hud didn't want any dinner?

ALMA
(dryly)
He's prettying up. Said he'd eat later.

LON

What's for dessert?

ALMA

You think a big freezerful of peach ice cream'll hold you?

LON

Boy, I been waitin' all winter for those locker-plant Alberta peaches.

ALMA
(grinning)
Is that what you been waiting all winter for, sugar? What about all those peachy pin-ups you keep hidden in with your shorts and socks?

LON

That's my private drawer! You stay out of there.

ALMA

I'm a girl, honey. They don't do a thing for me.
(back to the sink)
I'll dish out your ice cream and you have it on the front porch. It's cooler.

GRANDDAD

That'll be fine.

Lon lets Granddad go out first. Alma is standing all spraddle-legged as she bends to lift the freezer, and Lon gives her the hip as he goes by. But she straightens too quickly and he misses.

ALMA

Go on, before you wet your didy.

Lon smiles and follows the old man.

Hud's VOICE is suddenly heard from the top of the stairs.

HUD'S VOICE

Alma, get me a clean shirt.

ALMA
(calling back)
You're real big with Please and Thank You, aren't you?

HUD'S VOICE

Please get off your lazy butt and get me a clean shirt, thank you.

She wipes her hands on a dish towel and goes out.

INT. HUD'S BEDROOM
Hud is snapping a polishing rag over his boots as Alma enters with a freshly ironed shirt.

> ALMA
> I had a little trouble getting the lipstick out of this one.

> HUD
> Yeah? Well, let's try the brand you're wearin'. Maybe it'll wash out easier.

> ALMA
> *(calmly)*
> Let's not.

> HUD
> You're not gettin' any younger. What're you savin' it for?

> ALMA
> *(shortly)*
> Tabs are in the collar.

She goes out. Hud looks after her, beginning to be intrigued.

EXT. FRONT PORCH
Granddad is in a cord-bottomed chair, Lon on the steps below him. Both are quiet and reflective.

A whippoorwill SINGS out nearby.

> LON
> Hear the whippoorwill?

> GRANDDAD
> I think there's two of 'em.

> LON
> I've never seen one of those birds in my whole life. All you do is hear 'em call across the flat . . .

A calf BAWLS somewhere in the night. A big diesel truck GROWLS far off on the highway.

> GRANDDAD
> What're you thinkin' about, Lon?

LON

Oh . . . I don't know. Just lookin' up ahead, I guess. You know. To what's coming.

GRANDDAD

Thinkin' about your worries and your ambitions, are you?

LON

Yeah, that. And havin' a car of my own to tear around in . . . and girls . . .

GRANDDAD

I expect you'll have your share of what's good. A boy like you deserves it.

Lon looks at him gratefully.

GRANDDAD

Feels like it's gettin' to be my bedtime.

He takes out his old silver pocket watch and looks at it. Lon reaches across and points to the picture of a young man pasted inside the lid.

LON

My dad sure looks like his collar was chokin' him.

GRANDDAD

Those were his Sunday best.

LON

I don't remember him any.

GRANDDAD
(painfully)

I do.

Lon hesitates a moment.

LON

You don't carry a picture of Hud around with you.

GRANDDAD

No, I don't.

LON
(slowly)

But he's your son—same as my dad was.

GRANDDAD

Yes, he is.

LON
(pauses)
What're you holdin' against him, Granddad?

GRANDDAD
(flat)
He knows. And you don't need to.

He snaps the watch shut, as though closing a door on something. Alma comes out with a bowl of ice cream for each of them.

ALMA

Here you go.

GRANDDAD

Aren't you havin' any?

ALMA

Too many calories. I'm trying to lose a couple of pounds.

While the men begin to spoon their dessert, she wanders to the porch swing and sinks down with a sigh.

ALMA

If you don't mind, Mister Bannon, I'm going to leave the dishes for later. I've got to get off these feet.

GRANDDAD

Kitchen's your department, Alma.

ALMA

Well, I've seen enough of it for today.

She lights a cigarette. Hud comes out from the house and joins them. He helps himself to a spoonful of Lon's ice cream.

HUD

Hey, that's pretty good.

This time he takes the bowl and begins eating it himself.

GRANDDAD

Hud, you plannin' to go back into town tonight?

HUD

I didn't dress up to sit on this front porch and listen to the frogs mate.

GRANDDAD

I'd like for you to make it back here before morning. The vet'll be here early.

The swing SQUEAKS as Alma rocks back and forth, her handsome brown legs sprawled out carelessly. Both Hud and Lon watch her. She pulls at the front of her loose, floppy blouse.

ALMA

Whew. You can't get much air through this nylon.

LON

You ought to go around in a sarong, like they do in the South Seas.

ALMA
(dryly)
Yeah, that'd be a lot of laughs.

HUD

You're half native already. I haven't seen you in a pair of shoes since you came to work here.

ALMA

I wore 'em once. I think it was to get married in. White satin pumps.
(shrugs)
Don't have them anymore or the man either.

HUD

Well, I'm gonna hit for town. Alma, you wanta blow some foam off some beer?

ALMA

No, thanks. If I can ever get up out of this swing, I'm gonna set some biscuits and go to bed.

HUD
(drawling)
I'll settle for *half* of that action.

She glances at him coolly. He is grinning. Lon interrupts eagerly.

> LON
>
> I'll go with you, Hud.

> HUD
>
> What big deal have you got lined up in town—a Sno Cone or something?

> LON
> *(lamely)*
>
> Just thought I'd catch a ride with you.

> HUD
>
> All right, honcho. Come on. Let's make tracks.

> LON
> *(turns deferentially)*
>
> You didn't want me for anything, did you, Granddad?

> GRANDDAD
>
> No, you go along if you like. Just be careful.

Granddad stares at Hud.

> HUD
> *(to Lon)*
>
> You drive, sport.

He makes an elaborate gesture of handing the keys to Lon. The two men get in and the Cadillac wheels slowly out of the yard.

INT. CAR—MOVING SHOT

> LON
> *(puzzled)*
>
> What was that all about?

> HUD
>
> That's a story I'll tell you some day when I'm drunk.

Hud's manner has changed. He has become withdrawn, moody.

> HUD
>
> Come on, gig this thing a little, will you?

Lon accelerates. They go in silence. The boy automatically reaches into his shirt pocket and turns on his radio. The STRAINS of "Honey Love" fill the car.

>   HUD
>   *(irritably)*
> Kill that radio.

Lon turns it OFF. Another silence.

>   LON
> It's a lonesome ol' night, isn't it?

>   HUD
>   *(flat)*
> Aren't they all?

Both of them turn their heads to look across the prairie at the Zephyr.

REVERSE SHOT—THE ZEPHYR
The train flies by in the distance, the hundred lighted windows of the passenger cars vivid in the night. The whistle BLOWS, cutting across the dark prairie like the whistling train itself.

INT. CAR—MOVING SHOT

>   LON
> Boy, I love that sound. It goes right through me.

>   HUD
>   *(puncturing)*
> Scares the hell out of the cattle.

>   LON
> You know what trains always make me think about?

>   HUD
> No, but I got a strong feeling you're gonna tell me.

>   LON
>   *(backing off)*
> I guess I just like 'em, that's all . . .

The boy subsides, stealing a glance at his uncle now and then. The lights of Thalia are just ahead, bright against the dark sky.

Lon drives into the square, circles it, and parks in front of the light bulbs and cardboard posters of the picture show.

EXT. THALIA
They get out of the car. Hud takes the keys from Lon and pockets them.

The two men stop at a store window, where an elaborate saddle is on display.

> HUD
>
> Look at that Las Vegas saddle. You couldn't lift that hunk of junk on a horse with a crane.

> LON
>
> Yeah, it is pretty noisy.

Hud starts across the street and Lon lopes along at his side. Hud stops.

> HUD
>
> Where do you think you're goin'?

> LON
>
> Just taggin' along.

> HUD
>
> Not with me, you ain't. You go tie on a couple of Doctor Peppers. I'll see you.

Hud disappears into the bar without a backward glance and Lon is left alone on the curb, looking after him. As always, the boy is pulled two different ways: fear of Hud on the one hand, and a longing to associate himself with the swagger and maleness of his uncle's life. Lon goes toward the store.

EXT. STORE
A couple of old women are rocking on the porch, in front of the RC Cola thermometers and the Garrett snuff signs, as Lon comes ambling up the steps with nothing to do. He moseys inside.

INT. STORE
Lon twirls the paperback rack a time or two and idly picks up From Here to Eternity. *KIRBY, the proprietor, addresses him.*

> KIRBY
>
> Read that one?

> LON
> *(nodding)*
>
> Twice. That's about the best book you ever got on your paperback stand.

> KIRBY
>
> Pretty steamy, ain't it?

LON

Oh, I don't know. The people in it seem a lot like the ones I see.

KIRBY

Didya read the part where the sergeant gets her for the first time?

LON

Yeah, I read that part.

The boy is embarrassed. He puts the book down and takes another.

EXT. BAR—MOVING SHOT
Hud is just coming out as Lon approaches. The boy falls into step beside him.

HUD

I'm seein' an awful lot of you for one night.

LON

I'm just headed for the square, is all.
(after a moment)
Where're you headed?

HUD
(flatly)
Well, just to keep you up to date, I'm makin' my way to Missus Ruby Fletcher's house.
(glances at him)
I don't think that's a house you're likely to've heard very much about.

LON
(self-consciously)
I've heard some . . .
(then more strongly)
I'm out of my three-cornered pants, you know. I have been for some time.

HUD

What are you, hotrod? A big seventeen?
(then)
Now lemme see. When I was seventeen, I never got enough of anything. That was the summer you were born. Your ma

died and your daddy was feelin' pretty wild about things. We bought us a '27 Chevy, and kept it tied together with bailin' wire. We made every square dance and rodeo and honky-tonk in the country, and I don't know which we run the hardest—that car or the country girls that showed up at the dances. We do-si-doed and chased those girlish butts around many a circle that summer.

                    LON
I wouldn't mind going that route myself.

                    HUD
Come on along.

Lon shakes his head. It is not fear but a simple, young dignity that holds him back.

                    LON
No, I don't think so.

                    HUD
  All right.

INT. LON'S BEDROOM—DAY
Alma shakes the sleeping boy, trying to rouse him. He lies under a single sheet, dead to the world.

                    ALMA
Hey, wake up. Come on, Lonnie.
                    (he groans)
Come on, open your eyes. You gonna stay here till dinner time?

                    LON
Whaddaya want?

                    ALMA
I want you to get off the bed. I can't stand here wrestling around with you all morning.

                    LON
                    (grins slowly)
Why not? I kinda like it.

                    ALMA
I'll bet you do. But that's enough out of you now. Get up.

LON

Can't do that, Alma.

ALMA

Are you sleeping in the raw again?

LON

Uh-huh.

ALMA

I got two pair of nice ironed cotton pajamas in there. How come you're not using them?

LON

I don't know. They strangle me.
(lies in bed watching her)
What do you sleep in?

ALMA

In my own room, with the door locked.

LON

Ever wear those little shortie things?

ALMA

What kind of a question is that?

LON

Just wonder.

ALMA

Does your mind usually run in that direction?

LON

Yeah, it seems to.

ALMA

Boys with impure thoughts come out in acne, you know that?

LON

That's all bull, Alma.

ALMA

Keep it up, you'll see.

She goes out. Her VOICE calls back to him from the hall:

ALMA'S VOICE
Hurry up. The vet's coming this morning.

He lies blankly for a moment and then, as he remembers, he leaps out of bed and starts pulling on his jeans.

EXT. PASTURE—DAY
The heifer seems shrunken now, green flies getting what the buzzards could not. BURRIS and THOMSON, the vets, square-cut men with medical badges pinned to their jackets, hunker around the carcass with all the men from the ranch. Burris has rubber gloves on and is carefully cutting out the cow's tongue and putting it in a bottle he has in his bag.

BURRIS
Let's get away from this stink. I've got all I need. We can go to the shade and talk cool.

EXT. UNDER A TREE
as the party moves over under its branches. Granddad finds a little stick and begins to whittle. He sits with his brown hat pulled way down over his forehead, looking tired and old but determined.

BURRIS
Mister Bannon, I'm gonna ask you to get your cattle together. All of 'em. We're gonna have to make an inspection.

GRANDDAD
Inspection for what?

BURRIS
For what killed that heifer. I hope I'm wrong, but I'm very much afraid you've got the worst kind of trouble a cattle-man can have.
(pauses)
I think that cow died of hoof-and-mouth disease.

A silence falls. Hud is impassive, Lon drawn with tension.

GRANDDAD
(softly)
Oh, me. I never thought it would be nothin' like that.

HUD
(flat)
What're we in for? Let's have it.

                    BURRIS

You-all round up your herds. We're gonna have to take
some samples, bring in a few healthy calves and a couple of
horses from outside, infect them artificially, and then just
wait and see what happens.

                     HUD

I'll tell you what'll happen. They turn up sick and you kill
'em. That's right, isn't it, Mister?

                    BURRIS

If the calves turn up sick and the horses don't, it's hoof-and-
mouth. You got to. The last bad outbreak in the United
States, the government had to kill about 77,000 cattle, plus
that many sheep and goats, and even 20,000 deer. It's a
terrible thing.

                   GRANDDAD

I've just bought me twenty head of Mexican cows down
south. Could they be the bad ones?

                    BURRIS

Could be. If they were—you'll have to get rid of every cow
that's been in contact with 'em.

                   GRANDDAD

You're talkin' about all the animals I own.

                    BURRIS
                   (quietly)

I know I am.

                   (pauses)

I hope I'm wrong. I hope it turns out to be something else
so we won't ever have to talk about it again.

*He signals to Thomson. The two men shake hands with Granddad, nod to
the others, walk to the old Ford parked nearby. The men are silent as the vets
get in and drive across the pasture. Jesse is the first to speak.*

                    JESSE

Looks like I landed in the wrong place again.

Foreboding sits heavily on Granddad. Hud turns abruptly to Jesse and Jose.

                     HUD

You guys get on it. There's a fence to fix.

The cowhands look to Granddad. He nods and they go.

> HUD
> *(turning to Granddad)*
> How about that? You gonna have your cows shot on ac-
> count of a schoolbook disease? You gettin' that old, Homer?

> GRANDDAD
> I wonder if a long quarantine wouldn't satisfy them. Think
> they'd agree to that?

> HUD
> They don't need you to agree to *nothin'*. They're the law.
> You can agree with them till hell freezes over for all the
> good it'll do you.

> GRANDDAD
> That Mister Burris seemed like a reasonable man.
> *(pauses)*
> Do you think they'd come in and liquidate?

> HUD
> Hell, yes, they'll liquidate, if you got what they say you got.
> *(intensely)*
> Now you've had twenty-four of my thirty-four years workin'
> this place. And Daddy, you've had top-grade cheap labor. I
> shoveled manure out of the barns for you. You've had my
> callouses. For what? For your blessings the day I die?
> *(hard)*
> No, damn it. I want back out of this spread what I put into it.

> GRANDDAD
> You got a proposal to make to me, Hud?

> HUD
> Yeah. Get on the telephone tonight and sell every breed
> cow you own. They haven't got a chain on you yet.

Both Granddad and Lon stare at him incredulously.

> GRANDDAD
> Would that be your way of gettin' out of a tight?

> HUD
> I can ship the whole herd out before they begin the tests.

> GRANDDAD

You mean try and pass bad stuff off on my neighbors, who wouldn't even know what they were gettin'?

> HUD

All right, I'll take them out of the state, unload 'em up north before the news gets out.

> GRANDDAD

And take a chance on startin' an epidemic in this entire country?

> HUD

This whole country is run on epidemics—where've you been? Epidemics of big business price fixin' and crooked TV shows and souped-up expense accounts and income tax finaglin'. How many honest people do you know? Take the sinners away from the saints and you'll be lucky to end up with Abraham Lincoln.

> *(emphatically)*

I say let's put our bread in some of that gravy while it's still hot!

> GRANDDAD
> *(very quietly)*

You're an unprincipled man, Hud.

Hud sees that he has come up against rock. For the moment he retreats into what appears to be good humor.

> HUD
> *(drawling)*

Don't let that fuss you. You've got enough for both of us.

EXT. ROUND-UP—DAY
The men ride through the hot, weedy pastures, pushing the cows and calves out of the shady places where they are resting. There are four smaller pastures as well as the large one and they are all being systematically combed. The herd begins to grow as each man gathers another bunch out of the brush and throws it into the main body.

EXT. PASTURE
A nervous cow skitters away from the herd. Hud is on her in an instant, cutting his pony sharply, slapping the cow's flanks and maneuvering her back.

EXT. HORSE PASTURE TANK

The cows are being driven up the hill toward the house. The horses are lathered from the morning's work and the cows are too hot. The calves have their tongues out, dripping long white strings of slobber into the dust. Every minute or two the old cows try to stop and graze, but Lon whoops down on them and moves them on.

EXT. NEAR THE HOUSE

The cows are drifting into the big horse pasture tank. The men are as hot and droopy as the cattle. Yellow, choking dust rises in waves.

EXT. ROUND-UP

Jesse and Jose prowl through the heavy mesquite thickets. The work in here is harder; the cows hide and must be flushed out one at a time.

EXT. ROUND-UP

Lon trots along a brown shelving ridge, shoving through the thick weeds and the blooming green mesquites, throwing a bunch of cows into the main herd and then turning back for another.

EXT. TANK

Hud pushes a bunch down the brown sandy trail to a tank. The old cows wade in up to their bellies, while the big half-yearling calves bawl on the banks.

Hud pauses a moment to light a cigarette, sees something to his left and suddenly spurs over.

EXT. BENEATH A TREE

Granddad has dismounted for a moment to sink to the ground and rest, mopping his face with a large handkerchief. Hud rides up and looks down at him from his mount.

> GRANDDAD
> This afternoon's been a regular bitch.

> HUD
> Are you out of poop?

> GRANDDAD
> Just havin' a breather.

> HUD
> If it's too much for you, why don't you go back to the ranch and grab yourself a nap?

GRANDDAD
(quietly)
No. I'll hold up my end of it.

HUD
(a hint of respect)
Yeah, you would, even if it killed you.

Granddad rises without speaking, climbs a little laboriously into the saddle. Hud watches as he rides away, as if measuring him.

EXT. PASTURE—DAY
Granddad tops a hill. The red sun is dropping cleanly down the last few feet of sky. The pasture lies under the quietest, stillest light of day. Far below him, Jesse drives a herd. The old cows walk slowly, their red coats gray to the flank with dust, their heads low. Some still carry calves, their sides bulging like barrels.

Granddad turns away. He is all alone under the clear spread of light.

ANOTHER ANGLE
as the old man sees Lon coming toward him, driving two longhorn steers, the rangy bridle steers that belong to another time, another era.

LON
I found your longhorns out near Idiot Ridge.

GRANDDAD
The government's gonna have a time tryin' to inspect 'em.
Those big horns'll never go through a chute.

They fall still, watching the powerful, savage-looking steers.

LON
There aren't many left in this country, are there?

GRANDDAD
No, they're dyin' out. I just keep 'em for old times' sake.
Keep 'em to remind me how things was . . .
(pauses)
Everything we had came from their hides—our furniture,
our ropes, our clothes, our hats . . .

LON
(suddenly)
Granddad, let's turn 'em loose!

> GRANDDAD
> *(gently)*
Why, no, Lon. That wouldn't be the thing to do. They gotta go along with the rest.

Grandfather and grandson fall in between the two longhorns and move forward through the twilight, and Granddad says no more.

INT. MOVIE HOUSE—NIGHT
The lights are still on, the place a hubbub of young people. Lon slips back into his seat beside Granddad.

The old man is fast asleep, his head on his chest. Lon watches him quietly. Granddad comes awake with a start, smothers a jaw-breaking yawn.

> LON
I shouldn't've brought you tonight. Not after the day you put in.

> GRANDDAD
> *(grins)*
If the picture show is any good, I'll wake up, don't you worry.

Lon hands him a bag and they sit munching popcorn together. Just ahead of them, two adolescents neck exuberantly. Granddad's eyes twinkle.

> GRANDDAD
Looks like you're the only one around here who hasn't got someone whose knee you can pinch.

> LON
I can stand it.

> GRANDDAD
> *(sees another couple embrace)*
You wouldn't think they'd pay sixty-five cents to come here and do it. They can go up in a hay loft for nothin'.

The house darkens; the screen glows. A short subject comes on, a song accompanied by a bouncing ball. Granddad lustily joins in the singing. Lon looks at him and grins with pleasure.

INT. CAFÉ—NIGHT
Granddad and Lon are in a booth in the packed café. The boy is just about to bite into an enormous hamburger with all the trimmings.

GRANDDAD
You gonna get your mouth around all that?

LON
I'm gonna try.

Lon nods and accomplishes it. The old man looks around idly and catches sight of Hud coming in with Lily Peters.

GRANDDAD
Is that Truman Peters's wife with Hud?

LON
I think so. Want me to call him over?

GRANDDAD
No, we'll just leave him to his business.

Hud sees them, though, and comes over, dragging Lily by the hand. He is high.

HUD
Let's make a party out of this. Daddy, this not-too-natural blonde is Missus Truman Peters.

GRANDDAD
(politely)
How do you do?

LILY
Hello, Mister Bannon.

HUD
Wild Horse Homer Bannon, Lily. That's what they used to call him. And this gangly youth is my nephew Lon.
(he pushes his hat back on his head)
You may have just noticed that my daddy hasn't asked us to sit down. It's 'cause he doesn't want to socialize with me— he's a little fussy about the company he keeps . . . Yeah, you're a married woman, Lily. That doesn't go down very well with him. He's a man of high principles and what have you. He doesn't believe in any loose living at all. Isn't that right, Homer?

Granddad makes a spasmodic gesture, as if to ward off further talk, and a water glass goes over as he collapses.

LON

Granddad!

HUD

Homer, you okay?

GRANDDAD

Get me home, boys.

Lon is at Hud's side. They each take an arm and begin helping him out.

INT. PICKUP TRUCK—MOVING SHOT—NIGHT
Lon drives back home on the black, empty highway, Hud and Granddad up front with him. The old man is awake, his face looking thinner than it has, the short silver whiskers showing ragged against his skin.

GRANDDAD

Turn down that window a little, will you, Hud?
(Hud rolls it down)
That's good. Place back there seemed a little short of air.

LON

Maybe you got too much sun today.

GRANDDAD

Well, whatever. Anyway, there's no need to go pullin' such a long face about it. I'm better now.

LON

As soon as we get home, I'll fix you some Sal Hepatica.

GRANDDAD

Yeah, that'll settle me right down.

He puts his head back and closes his eyes. He is asleep in an instant, weaving slightly with the jostling of the truck.

LON

He dropped right off.

Lon watches the old man in the mirror. Hud remains silent. Far off on the prairie there is the hot ROLL of distant thunder.

LON

He's beginnin' to look kind of worn out, isn't he? Sometimes I forget how old he is. I guess I just don't want to think about it.

> HUD
Time you started.

> LON
> *(unnerved)*
Well, I know he's gonna die some day. I know that much.

> HUD
He is.

> LON
It makes me feel like somebody dumped me into a cold river.

> HUD
It happens to everybody. Dogs, horses, men. Nobody gets out of life alive.

EXT. BANNON HOUSE
as the truck rolls to a stop. Granddad comes awake again and Lon helps him out. Hud comes around to assist him.

> HUD
I'll give you a hand inside.

> GRANDDAD
Lon'll look after me. Good night, Hud.

> HUD
Suit yourself.

He steps aside. The other two enter the house, leaving him alone. A dog YAPS, stranded somewhere out in the coyote country. Hud goes to the windmill and lets the faucet run till the cold deep well water comes GURGLING up through the pipes. He bends over and takes a long drink. There is a BLAZE of light in the yard as the bunkhouse door opens and Alma emerges.

> ALMA
I enjoyed the game, boys. You can have another shot at me next pay day.

She closes the door and starts across the dark yard to her cabin.

INT. ALMA'S CABIN

She puts on the light as she enters. She turns down her bed, yawns, begins to undress.

She is suddenly aware of Hud, leaning against the screen door. She buttons up the front of her blouse again quickly.

HUD

Got a cigarette? I'm out.

She hesitates a moment, looking at him.

ALMA

Wait a minute.

She turns aside for her purse, begins digging in it.

HUD
(wryly)

I wish you wouldn't keep me hangin' around on the door-step. Makes me feel like I'm sellin' something.

ALMA
(slowly)

All right. Come in.

He opens the screen door and enters. She hands him the pack.

ALMA

They're a little squashed.

HUD

They'll do.

He lights up and then looks around.

HUD

I see you've got this place fixed up some.

ALMA

I try.

HUD

It looks pretty good—except your sweet potato plant over there has got the blight.

ALMA

I can't seem to get one started.

HUD

They need a lot of encouraging—just like the rest of us.

                          ALMA
                          (dryly)
I'll keep it in mind.

                          (then)
Could I have a match?

Hud tosses her a book of matches then gives himself a tour of her cabin.

                          HUD
Well, what have we got here? Jiffy portable hair dryer. A
sifter with a triple screen. Automatic toaster. What have
you been doin'? A little rustlin' down at the five and dime?

                          ALMA
I go in for those prize contests. "That Shine-It Shampoo
changed my life." You know, they give free two-week trips
to Europe, but I end up with the fountain pens and the
Japanese binoculars.

                          HUD
I won me a turkey raffle once, but it was fixed. I got to be
pretty friendly with one of them gals picking the numbers.

                          ALMA
It figures.

Hud takes a chair, tilts it against the wall.

                          HUD
How much did you take the boys for?

                          ALMA
Twenty dollars and some change.

                          HUD
You're a dangerous woman to have around.

                          ALMA
                          (flatly)
Well, I'm a good poker player.

                          HUD
You're a good cook, too. Good laundress. Good housekeeper. What else are you good at?

                              ALMA
Taking care of myself.

                              HUD
You shouldn't have to, a woman who looks like you do.

                              ALMA
That's what my ex-husband used to tell me, before he took
my wallet and my gasoline credit card and left me stranded
in a downtown motel in Albuquerque, New Mexico.

                              HUD
Why'd he take to the hills? Did you wear curlers to bed or
something?

                              ALMA
Ed's a gambler. He's probably up at Vegas or Reno right
now, dealing at night and losing it all back in the daytime.

                              HUD
Why, that man sounds no better than a heel.

                              ALMA
                             (flat)
Aren't you all?

                              HUD
Now, honey, don't go shootin' all the dogs just cause one's
got fleas.

                              ALMA
I was married to Ed for six years, and the only thing he was
ever good for was to scratch my back where I couldn't reach
it.

                              HUD
                            (lazily)
Still got that itch?

                              ALMA
                    (she is always honest)
Off and on.

                              HUD
Well, let me know when it starts to bother you.

He tilts forward with a crack of the chair, gets up and goes out. Again Alma begins to undress, moving slowly, troubled.

EXT. THE CHUTE—DAY
The cattle are milling and stirring up dust in the big pen as the men from the ranch stand outside the chute with the vets, ready to begin.

BURRIS
What we're doing, Mr. Bannon, is injecting these cows and horses with specimens from your herd. In three to six days we should know what we want to know.

Granddad sits on the fence to watch and gives the signal. Hud runs a few cows into a little crowding pen, Lon and Jesse take over to put them into the chute, Jose works at the other end, letting the cattle out when the vets are done. The vets are dressed in gray coats and have a vast array of bottles and jars set out.

There are WHOOPS and SHOUTS from the men. It is a mean, tiresome job, getting the cows to take the tight squeeze. Lon is soon covered with dust and hoarse from yelling. The cattle kick and spin and BELLOW, starting in and backing out, refusing to move.

Branches and creeks and streams of sweat run out from under their shirtsleeves and hatbands; there are dark muddy brown spots in the circles of dirt under their eyes. And thick, obscuring dust rises as always, as if there were a great fan in the bottom of the pen, blowing it up.

Lon tries to spin away and a large cracked hoof catches him on the hip, hitting his chaps with a SPLAT. He is knocked against the fence, splintering it, and then falls in the sandy pen, out cold. Granddad drops inside immediately; Hud is at his side. They dodge the horns, scooping up the boy between them, and scramble back with him up and over to safety.

EXT. OUTSIDE THE CHUTE
Lon comes to, sitting with his back against the red plank railing of the scales. Granddad is wiping his forehead with a wet handkerchief and Hud stands nearby watching.

GRANDDAD
You all right, Lon?
(the boy nods weakly)
She kicked you into the fence. You skint your head a little on the pipe.

> (*smiles*)

Boy, you caught a lick.

Lon nods with a sickly little grin.

> HUD

You better get back to work. The cowboys'll be on you for
a week if you quit because you dented your head a little.

> GRANDDAD

No need to rush him.

*But Lon struggles manfully to his feet. He has the weak trembles in his legs
and suddenly flops over again. Hud picks him up and throws him over his
shoulder.*

> HUD

You've had it, fantan.

> GRANDDAD

Get him to bed.

MOVING SHOT
as Hud lugs Lon toward the house.

> HUD

All this time I thought you were skinny. But you weigh a ton.

> LON
> (*woozily*)

I can't get my head right . . . Hud, I think I'm gonna lose
my breakfast.

> HUD

Not all over me, you're not! You just hold your fire till we
get into the house.

INT. HALLWAY—BANNON HOUSE
*Alma sees them from the kitchen and comes running, flour up her arms to
her elbows. She grabs Lon by the arm and looks into his face anxiously.*

> ALMA

Sugar, you're white as a sheet!

> LON
> (*weakly*)

Sure I'm white—you got flour all over me.

ALMA

What happened?

HUD

One of the cows cuddled up to him.

ALMA

Shouldn't a doctor look at him?

HUD

What? Pay five bucks for some iodine and an aspirin? He'll mend.

He hikes Lon up again and carries him up the stairs.

INT. LON'S BEDROOM
Hud brings the boy over to his bed and drops him on it.

HUD

That's as far as I go. I draw the line at bedpans.

LON

Thanks, Hud . . .

HUD

You can goldbrick for the rest of the day. Just don't try to stretch it into two.

He waves at the boy and goes out. Lon lies lathered in a pool of his own sweat. He can hear the cattle BAWLING from the lots. Alma enters with a pitcher.

ALMA

Let's get your shoes off.

She pulls them off and then sits on the bed beside him, handing him a glass.

ALMA

Cold lemonade.

The boy struggles up to drink it and she puts her arm around him to help.

ALMA

Don't swallow the seeds.

Lon looks around for a place to spit them and she holds out her palm.

ALMA

Here.
(as he hesitates)
Come on. They're only lemon seeds.

He tries to be delicate about getting rid of them in her hand and she smiles. He finishes and falls back. She holds the cold glass to his forehead.

ALMA

Better?
(he nods)
You ought to try and doze off now.

He puts his hand over hers.

LON

Gee, you're cool. Smell of lemon.

The boy suddenly lurches over and buries his head in her lap.

LON
(yearning)

Alma . . .

ALMA

What is it, sugar?

LON

You're really beautiful.

ALMA
(soothingly)

Sure I am.

LON

You're one of the best people there ever was. You're good
to me, Alma. In fact you're good, period.

ALMA

All right. You be good too and go to sleep.

His eyes close but he still holds onto her hand. She remains quietly beside him.

EXT. BIG PASTURE—DAY
Late in the afternoon, the sky a country of changing colors, red in the west,

blue in the east. Jesse hammers a large sign into the ground. It faces the road so that passing motorists can see it: "QUARANTINE."

EXT. SMALL PASTURE
Jose drags a chain across the gate posts and locks the gate. Here too a fresh-painted sign warns, "QUARANTINE." Two hawks glide low over the pasture, dipping and swooping.

EXT. ANOTHER PASTURE
Hud hammers a "QUARANTINE" sign to the fence.

The hawks sail past, almost steady in the air. Dozens of feeding jackrabbits break before them, zigzagging off to one side and stopping, their long ears folded against their heads.

EXT. FRONT PORCH
Lon emerges into the white heat, the oppressive stillness of the day. Hud and Granddad are on the porch. Something in the heavy inertia of the two men puts a lid on his good spirits. He notices that Hud is already drinking.

> LON

'Morning, everybody.

> GRANDDAD

How are you today, Lonnie?

> LON

Great. Just great.
> *(he tries to fill up the silence)*
Boy, have I been sawin' wood up there. Looks like I slept around the clock.

Hud gives him an extremely sour look. Lon claps his hands together energetically.

> LON

I feel almost like workin' for a change. What d'ya got for me? Patch up a little fence, pull you some weeds, work a few calves?

> GRANDDAD
> *(heavily)*
I don't guess we'll do much of anything. I don't see any sense in wastin' work until I find out about my cattle.

                              HUD
                          (roughly)
Yeah, we're gonna roll over and play dead and let 'em
shovel dirt in our faces.

                           GRANDDAD
If I don't get a bill of health on these cattle, we are just
about dead.

                              HUD
Dead *broke.* We've been breeding and crossbreeding this
beef all our lives, to get us the best stock in the country,
and we're gonna end up with the government payin' us four
bits on the dollar for 'em. Poor but honest, that's us.

                           GRANDDAD
We're not sure of anything yet. We're just gonna have to sit
and wait it out.

                              HUD
Well, don't get sores on your butts doin' it!

*He scoops up his bottle and goes inside. It is quiet. Granddad seems
fatigued by worry. Lon sits on the steps below Granddad. He fumbles in his
shirt pocket and turns on his transistor. Rock and roll BLARES out—the
tune is "Bonaparte's Retreat."*

                           GRANDDAD
                          (shortly)
I could do without that noise, Lon.

*Lon turns it OFF, scratches himself nervously. He takes out his pocket knife
and begins flipping it idly into the flower bed.*

                           GRANDDAD
Go stretch your legs, will you?

*Lon is a little startled by the edginess in the old man's voice. He folds up the
knife apologetically and wanders away.*

EXT. BACK PORCH
*Alma is spreading a piece of cheesecloth over the top of an old milk strainer,
a large bucket of milk beside her. She HEARS the clatter of hoofs and looks
up to see Lon riding away from the house, bareback, on a large stallion. She
watches the lonely figure retreating, and then resumes her work, lifting the*

heavy bucket and pouring. The milk runs in a swirling white stream, leaving little flecks of dirt and manure stuck to the damp cheesecloth.

There is a COMMOTION in the kitchen behind her, a banging of cabinet doors.

HUD'S VOICE

Where's that bottle?

A moment later he appears on the back porch.

HUD

I'm missin' a bottle of Jack Daniels. I had it stashed in the cupboard in there.

ALMA

You drank it.

HUD

When?

ALMA

Instead of dinner, Wednesday night.

HUD

I don't remember.

ALMA

If you think I've been nipping at it, I don't drink anything but Tokay wine.

HUD

And I bet you keep your little finger crooked while you're doin' it.

ALMA

Why don't you stick your head under the pump and sober up for lunch?

HUD
(drawling)

Don't you find me in control of myself?

ALMA

Well, I'd hate to see you walk a straight line.

HUD

That's easy.

He takes three steps forward and pulls her up off the seat and into his arms. He kisses her roughly and it is a moment before she can wrench away.

> ALMA
> *(coolly)*

I don't like sudden passes.

> HUD
> *(lazily)*

Well, we'll ease into it then. There's another one comin' up on your right.

He bends and kisses her on the neck. His lips are still touching her when she speaks.

> ALMA
> *(quietly)*

Don't you ever ask?

> HUD
> *(shakes his head)*

The only question I ask any woman is, "What time's your husband comin' home?"

He kisses the other side of her neck. His hands caress her arms.

> HUD
> *(abruptly)*

Well, honey, what's keepin' you? You're over the age of consent, aren't you?

> ALMA
> *(flatly)*

Way over.

> HUD

Then let's get our shoelaces untied, what d'ya say?

> ALMA

I'd say I've been asked with a little more finesse in my time.

> HUD

Well, I wouldn't want to come on crude, no ma'am. You want the full treatment, you'll get it. I'll bring you a two-pound box of candy. Maybe a bottle of perfume from the drug store.

ALMA

How about some colored beads and wampum?

HUD
(nods)
Sure. Whatever it takes to make you trade.

ALMA

No, thanks. I've done my time with one cold-blooded bastard. I'm not looking for another.

HUD
(evenly)
It's too late, honey. You've already found him.

He takes a few of the raw peas and pops them into his mouth. Chewing on them like nuts he saunters back into the house.

INT. KITCHEN
The three men are finishing dinner, everyone but Hud under a sense of strain. Alma seems withdrawn, a little wary of Hud as she passes him to clear up.

ALMA
You hardly touched your plate, Mister Bannon.

GRANDDAD
(wearily)
Nothin' to do with your cookin', Alma. Just not too hungry.

LON
(after a pause)
Any word from the vets?

GRANDDAD
No, they're takin' their own sweet time about it.

HUD
Well, I ain't goin' to sit around here and stew. The Kiwanis are waitin' for me.

LON
You gonna be in that pig scramble tonight, Hud?

HUD
(in a good humor)
Yeah, I'm gonna try and make the Bannons look good for a change.

> *(pushes back from the table)*

You honchos wanta come and sit in the cheerin' section? There's plenty of room.

He pauses beside Alma on his way out.

HUD

It's Ladies' Night. You might qualify.

With that he grins and goes. They sit quietly until they HEAR his car start and roar off toward the highway. Granddad sighs a little.

LON

You know, that's the first time in my life Hud ever asked me to go anywhere. I wonder why he did it?

GRANDDAD

Lonesome, I imagine. Just tryin' to scare up a little company.

LON

Hud lonesome? Why he can get more women company than anybody around here.

GRANDDAD

That ain't necessarily much. It ain't necessarily company, neither. Women just like to be around something dangerous part of the time.

> *(pause)*

Even Hud can get lonesome once in a while.

LON

I wouldn't mind watchin' him chase those squeelers.

GRANDDAD
(quietly)

Then we'll go in.

ALMA
(flatly)

I'll stay home. I don't like pigs.

EXT. ARENA—PIG CHASE—NIGHT
A teenage dance contest is just coming to a close.

ANNOUNCER

That's it, ladies and gentlemen . . . you've already seen one kind of twistin'—now you're about to see another. We've got ten able-bodied men gonna tie themselves in knots trying to catch ten of the fastest greased pigs you've ever seen in your life. The first man who catches his pig and brings it back to this little square here in front of the judges' stand is gonna be the winner. If you boys will come on in, we'll get this thing started.

Stripped to their undershirts, the contestants jump into the arena. Hud is among them.

ANNOUNCER
You guys got the pigs ready down there?

ANNOUNCER'S ASSISTANT
You bet.

And the pigs are led into the arena.

ANNOUNCER
All right, boys. Now, when I say three, we'll go. Onc . . . two . . . three, go!

The chase is on. Pigs slither through the contestants' hands as the crowd CHEERS; Lon and Granddad are part of the audience. Hud catches and loses his pig, falls into the mud, becomes more and more soiled as the men trip over each other, head each other off—it's a football game with swine for balls. Just as one man tackles and holds his prey, Hud comes along, pulls the pig out of his grasp, and drags it to the winner's square.

ANNOUNCER
It looks like we've got a winner—Hud Bannon. Hud, that pig looks about as dirty as you do.

The crowd LAUGHS.

ANOTHER ANGLE
The contest is over; people are milling about, leaving. Hud walks up to Lon and Granddad, wiping himself off with a towel.

GRANDDAD
I wish I could still get around the way you do, Hud.

LON
Boy, you sure do churn up that dust.

                    HUD
Well, I'm gonna kick up a little more dust before the night's
over.
                    (casually)
Anybody interested?

                    GRANDDAD
That's enough excitement for me, I guess. I'll be headin'
back.
                    (turns to the boy)
Lon?

                    LON
It's kinda early, I might just hang around with Hud a while.

                    GRANDDAD
                    (nods)
I'll leave the door open for you.

*He walks through the crowd, tall and straight. Lon feels a momentary pang
of guilt at deserting him but shrugs it off and looks at Hud expectantly.*

                    HUD
Hitch up your pants, fantan. I'm gonna get cleaned up, then
I'll buy you a drink.

INT. BAR
*The place is a beehive. A cowboy with a little too much spirit has his rope
and starts to make a loop, but his buddies swarm over him before he can do
any damage.*

*Hud and Lon find seats and a waitress brings two beers. Hud pulls a pint
bottle wrapped in a paper bag from his pocket and pours a shot into his beer.
He looks across at Lon.*

                    HUD
You want to put a little kick in that?

                    LON
Sure. Okay.

                    HUD
Never had any before, have you?

                    LON
I can handle it.

Hud pours the boilermaker and they drink. Lon does himself credit by not gagging. Then he leans back under the sign which forbids minors, now totally ignored, and looks around. A girl, MYRA BURSALL, sitting near the jukebox, catches his attention.

HUD

You found something?

LON

Kind of a pretty girl.

HUD
(smiles slightly)
Well, don't let me cramp you.

LON

I couldn't make any kind of a move at her.

HUD

Why? You're not nailed down, are you?

LON

That's what I call a woman-and-a-half.

HUD

You're not a bad-lookin' kid. Damp down that cowlick a little, button your shirt up over your Adam's apple, and you might just make out.

LON

I wouldn't mind driving her the long way home.

HUD

You oughta take a crack at it.
(pauses)
Get all the good you can out of seventeen, 'cause it wears out in a hell of a hurry.

LON

My trouble is I gotta like a girl a lot, before I can work up to anything. I mean like her as a person.

HUD

Fantan, you're a regular idealist.

LON

What's wrong with that?

                          HUD
                    (a slight smile)
I don't know. I've never tried it.

                          LON
I suppose you think I'm a jerk.

                          HUD
What do you care what I think?

                          LON
                    (quietly)
I guess it'll hand you a laugh, but I do.

                          HUD
                    (noncommittally)
Well, you have another drink, and I'll have another drink,
and before you know it we'll work up some real family
feeling here.

*There is no getting through to him on this level. Lon falls silent, holds out his
glass. Hud refills it and the boy takes a deep drink.*

                          LON
                    (suddenly)
I'm gonna shove some change in the jook.

He goes to the machine.

INT. NEAR THE JUKEBOX
*Lon passes the girl cautiously, stealing a look. He makes his selections,
presses the plungers. A Kitty Wells recording BEGINS. Myra sways to the beat
of the music. Lon gives the girl another shy, hurried glance, and CHARLIE
TUCKER, sitting with her, sees it and becomes annoyed.*

                          CHARLIE
What're you gawkin' at?

                          LON
Who? Me?

                          CHARLIE
I don't like fresh kids!

                          LON
Nobody's gettin' fresh, mister, that I know about.

CHARLIE

I think I'll take you out in the alley and jar some of your teeth loose.

Tucker rises angrily. Hud is suddenly standing there.

HUD
(pleasantly)

Are you havin' words with this youngster about something?

CHARLIE

I'm about to put him into the hospital!

HUD

Is that so? Is he botherin' you in any way?

CHARLIE

He's botherin' *her,* that's who he's botherin'!

HUD
(to the girl)

You didn't offer him a little encouragement by any chance, did you, young lady?

MYRA
(hotly)

No!

HUD
(mildly)

That's funny. I was sittin' clear across the room, and I got a little encouraged. Must be the way you move around inside that dress.

CHARLIE

All right, wise guy. I'll take you instead!

HUD

Oh, I don't wanta be hoggish. You want a piece of it, Lon?

Lon nods, white in the face. Tucker looks away from Hud to see the boy's reaction, and the instant he is off guard Hud belts him.

Lon steps forward determinedly but Hud holds out a detaining hand.

HUD

Wait your turn, I'm not finished.

But Lon does not wait, for Tucker is coming back with a bottle. Lon leaps to grab the man's hand, holding on like a terrier, while Hud rocks him again. The cowboys at the nearby tables whoop and wade in and it becomes a free-for-all, Hud and Lon in the middle of it, having the time of their lives.

EXT. YARD—BANNON HOUSE—NIGHT
The house in the background is dark and quiet. Hud has left the HEAD-LIGHTS of the car on so they can see to wash their battered faces at the horse trough. The brawl, the liquor, the camaraderie with Hud have all been tonic to the boy.

> LON
> That's what I call one hell of a night. I could do that about six times a week.

> HUD
> You don't win 'em all, you know.

> LON
> I would if you were backin' me all the time. Boy, that would make a combination, wouldn't it? Nobody'd ever mess with the Bannons, that's for sure.

> HUD
> Yeah, it felt like old times for a while tonight. Your dad and I used to take 'em on of a Saturday night.

> LON
> What kind of a man was he?

> HUD
> Norman?
> *(slowly)*
> He was the kind of a man who left his loose change out on top of the bureau, when I was a kid, so I could swipe some of it. Let me take a girl away from him once in a while, like I'd done it on my own.
> *(pauses)*
> He was bigger'n you are, had a bigger wallop, but I'll tell you something—when you're not being' a pain in the tail, you remind me a lot of him.

> LON
> I do?

HUD

Yeah. You sure do.

LON

Then how come you and me don't hit it off so good?

HUD

I got short arms.

Hud and Lon splash each other playfully with water from the trough.

HUD

Hell, ain't never been anybody like old Norman. Never will be. He was one way-out boy—thinking he could hear the grass grow. He got me to go down to this pasture one night to listen. After three, four hours just nippin' away at that bottle to keep the dew off us, I swore I could hear it too.
   (watches Lon thoughtfully as he continues)
That was the night I racked up the car. Wound up on Samson Creek Bridge. He died in half an hour and I didn't even have a mark on me . . . Yeah, I wonder if your daddy's hearing the grass now, growing up over his grave.
   (pauses)
That story ought to cool you off some.

LON

It doesn't.

Despite himself, Hud is relieved to find the boy's admiration for him unchanged. He shakes his head with mock rue.

HUD

Fantan, you're either soft-hearted or soft-headed, I don't know which.

INT. HALL
Granddad is coming down the stairs as they enter. His eyes go to Lon, unsteady on his feet, his shirt in tatters, a handkerchief wrapped around his fist. He does not speak for a moment.

GRANDDAD

All right. He's gotten you drunk. What else has he given you a taste for?

LON
(placating)
All we had was a couple of drinks, Granddad.

HUD
I don't remember you bein' a teetotaler.

GRANDDAD
(flat)
I drink. I don't object to his havin' whiskey.

*Lon sobers up in a hurry. There is something hard and uncompromising in
the old man's voice.*

HUD
Well, somethin' seems to be eatin' your liver.

GRANDDAD
You, Hud. Like always.

There is a slight pause.

LON
What are you climbin' on Hud for?

GRANDDAD
(slowly)
You think a lot of Hud, do you? You think he's a real man.
(his eyes go to Hud)
Well, you're bein' took in.

HUD
You listen to this, hotrod. I'm his son. He knows me.

GRANDDAD
I know you. You're smart. You've got your share of guts.
You can talk a man into trustin' you and a woman into
wantin' you.

HUD
Then I've got it made, haven't I?

GRANDDAD
To hear you tell it.

HUD
Why the hell don't you really get it off your chest! What you've got against me is what I did to Norman!

GRANDDAD
You were drunk and careless of your brother.

HUD
You've had fifteen years to get over it. That's half my life.

GRANDDAD
That's not our quarrel and never has been.

HUD
The hell it isn't!

GRANDDAD
No, boy. I was sick of you a long time before that.

It brings Hud up short. He pauses thoughtfully.

HUD
Well, isn't life full of surprises? All along I thought it was because of what I did to my big brother.

GRANDDAD
I took that hard, but I buried it.

HUD
All right. I'll bite. What turned you sour on me? Not that I give a damn.

GRANDDAD
Just that, Hud. You don't give a damn.
(pauses)
That's all. That's the whole of it.
(as Hud stares at him)
You still don't get it, huh?
(pauses again)
You don't care for people. You don't give a damn about them.

LON
(painfully)
Granddad—

The old man glances at the boy, pawn in the struggle.

> GRANDDAD
> *(slowly)*
> You got all that charm going for you, and it makes the
> youngsters want to be like you. That's the shame of it,
> 'cause you don't value nothin', you don't respect nothin',
> you keep no check on your appetites at all.
> *(flat)*
> You live just for yourself—and that makes you not fit to
> live with.

A pause.

> HUD
> Well, my momma loved me, but she died.

*He turns and goes out of the room. The rawness of the quarrel lies heavy on
Granddad. Lon breaks the silence.*

> LON
> Why pick on Hud? He isn't the only one. Just about every-
> body around here is like him, one way or another.

> GRANDDAD
> That's no cause for rejoicin', is it, Lonnie?
> *(goes on almost to himself)*
> . . . Little by little, the look of the country changes, because
> of the men we admire . . .

> LON
> *(awkwardly)*
> I still think you nailed him pretty hard . . .

> GRANDDAD
> Did I? Maybe. Old people get as hard as their arteries
> sometimes.
> *(he looks thoughtfully at Lon)*
> You're just gonna have to make up your own mind one day.
> About what's right and what's wrong.

*Lon nods. The old man goes up the stairs to his room, leaving Lon alone in
the hall.*

INT. KITCHEN
Hud is pawing in the breadbox as Lon enters. The scene with his father has plummeted Hud into one of his dark and dangerous moods.

                    HUD
Where's that high-paid housekeeper of ours? I want somethin'
to eat and I don't want any hesitatin' about it.

                    LON
                (gingerly)
It's late, Hud. She's asleep.

                    HUD
Well, ain't that just keen. Payin' her money to sleep when
I'm starvin' to death.

                    LON
I could fry you up an egg sandwich.

                    HUD
Forget it.

He chops two slices of bread and begins slamming a sandwich together. He turns suddenly on Lon.

                    HUD
Get your tail out of here. I can't think with you standin'
around.

                    LON
What're you cookin' up, Hud?

                    HUD
Wait and see. It's gonna knock some people on their tails,
and you might be one of 'em.

*Hud is too wild acting to fool with and Lon leaves. The LIGHTS in the hall
go out; there is a TREAD on the stairs. Hud remains in the kitchen,
thinking.*

EXT. RODEO ARENA—DAY
*The bulls and the bucking stock are being unloaded for the rodeo. In the
background, the warped, unpainted boards of the bleachers are beginning to
be filled with spectators.*

Lon and his friend Hermy sit on the fence watching the bulls being prodded out of a truck into the narrow chute and the winding maze of the holding pen. Hermy has a large contestant's number pinned to the front of his shirt.

> LON
> *(as a humpbacked bull passes beneath them)*

He means trouble . . .

> HERMY
> *(nervously)*

I kinda wish I'd stayed out of this bull riding.

> LON

From the look of them, you're not gonna be riding very far.

> HERMY

Thanks, buddy . . .
> *(then, reluctantly)*

Well, I better go check my gear.

> LON

Never mind your gear. You ought to go check your head.

Hermy slips off the fence and goes. Lon sits alone, watching a pretty cowgirl, one of the preliminaries, lope her painthorse around and around in circles in the main arena.

> HUD
> *(to Hermy)*

That bull's gonna eat you up.

ANOTHER ANGLE
as Hud comes up to his nephew. He is expansive, full of good spirits.

> HUD

Is that the best seat you could buy for this show?

> LON

They're gettin' two bucks for those bleachers over there.

> HUD

Well, be my guest.

He peels off some bills and gives them to the boy. Lon is surprised.

> LON

This is ten dollars, Hud.

> HUD
> *(grins)*

It's good. I didn't print it.

> LON

Well, thanks . . .

> HUD

Stick with me, honcho. You're gonna have your jeans full of change.

> LON

How come?

> HUD

Well, I'll tell you. I put on my dark blue business suit this morning, and I saw me a lawyer. You know they got a law says when old folks can't cut the mustard anymore, you can make them let go—whether they like it or not.

Lon comes down off the fence and stands before him.

> LON

What're you pullin' on Granddad now?

> HUD
> *(slowly)*

Something pretty raw, kid.

> LON

It sounds like it.
> *(suddenly thrusts the money back at Hud)*
Take your dough. I don't want it.

> HUD

Don't look down your nose at me, sonny. I'm gonna get old too some day, and I don't aim to end up on county relief, gettin' handed a bowl of soup and two cigarettes a day if I behave myself.
> *(intensely)*
I want what I worked for. I got a right to it. You see, honcho, if you don't look out for yourself, the only helping hand they'll ever give you is when they lower that box.

He pulls the boy toward him roughly, stuffs the money back in Lon's shirt pocket, and then turns and strides away. Troubled, Lon watches him go.

INT. HUD'S BEDROOM
Granddad enters as Hud, lying on his bed, watches TV.

GRANDDAD

Hud?

HUD

You're up awful late.

GRANDDAD

I've got a lot on my mind.

HUD

Come on in. Get a load off your feet.

Granddad closes the door.

HUD

Did you talk to the vets?

GRANDDAD

I talked to 'em, but I didn't get a whole lot of information out of 'em.

HUD

You didn't expect to, did you? When a government man wants you to know something, he'll call you, or else send you a telegram.

GRANDDAD

He said they were watchin' the test animals pretty close, but hadn't nothin' showed up yet.
(pauses)

Hud?

HUD

Yes, sir?

GRANDDAD

What's this tricky deal you're up to? Lon tells me you're tryin' to pull the rug out from under me.

HUD

That's right.

He looks at his father for a moment.

HUD

I haven't got all the rough edges ironed out yet, but I can give you an idea. The main thing is you, old man. You're too old to make the grade. Whether they liquidate us or not, when this thing is over you might as well get you a rocking chair so you'll be out of my way.

GRANDDAD

What in hell do you mean?

HUD

When a man your age goes off and buys a bunch of sick Mexican cows, it means he's over the hill. You've got the incompetence, Dad, and Hotrod here's too young to take over. So I might get the court to appoint me guardian of your property, I don't know. But if I don't get it one way, I'll get it another.

GRANDDAD

Why, you're badly mistaken about all this. I'll be the only one runs this ranch while I'm above ground. After that you might get some of it, I don't know. But you can't get control of this place no way in the world.

HUD

Don't go makin' any bets on that.

GRANDDAD
(slowly)

Maybe I treated you too hard. I don't doubt I made some mistakes. A man don't always do what's right.

HUD

Why, Daddy, you *never* been wrong. You've been handin' down the ten tablets of the law from whatever little hill you could find to climb up ever since I was a kid. Hell, you were Wild Horse Homer Bannon in those days, handin' out Scripture and verse like you made it up yourself.
(flat)

So I just naturally had to go bad, in the face of so much good.

GRANDDAD

Hud, how'd a man like you come to be a son to me?

Granddad storms out of Hud's room and into his own. Hud follows him as far as the hall.

HUD

That's easy. I wasn't no bundle left on your doorstep!

Granddad slams his door.

HUD
(continuing, louder)

You got the same feelings below your belt as any other man—that's how you got stuck with me for a son, whether you like it or not.

Hud charges out of the house past Lon, who has been listening at the other end of the hall.

EXT. YARD

as Hud comes CLATTERING down the back steps, hardly seeing where he goes. The big galvanized milk cans are in his way and he kicks them aside angrily. There is a grating metallic CRASH as they go spinning in the yard, bumping and CLASHING.

Hud stops, not knowing which way to go. He stands shifting back and forth on his feet, like a bull that has been crowded too close.

The LIGHT goes on in Alma's cabin and she appears framed in the open doorway, alarmed by the raucous NOISE. Hud lifts his head and sees her and turns to lurch toward her. He comes face to face with her, and she shows sudden fear.

He puts the heel of his hand just below her neck and shoves hard. She staggers back into the cabin with an involuntary gasp. He follows.

EXT. YARD

Lon runs across the yard. He flings open the door of the cabin.

INT. ALMA'S CABIN

As Lon comes rushing in, he is struck almost immediately with enormous force. Hud has turned away from the bed with blind instinct and hits him flush in the jaw, sending him skidding across the floor. Lon ends up crumpled against the wall, and Hud looks down at him blankly, as though he does not recognize him. Then it seems he does.

Blood is coming from the corner of Alma's mouth. Hud grabs her ankle and pulls her closer to him. She jabs at him, choking for air, and he falls across her twisting legs and tries to catch her hand.

A sudden silence falls. Something seems to flicker in Hud and then die out. He is at the end of his violence. He moves away, staggering a little, looks for the door, and then goes lurching out.

ANOTHER ANGLE
Alma lies on the bed with her head in her hands. Lon comes over, awkward with dismay and tenderness. He has trouble speaking.

> LON
> *(as though pleading with her)*
> He was just so drunk, Alma. Did he hurt you? Should I take you to town? Do you want a doctor or anything?

> ALMA
> No. Get out of here.

The boy leaves the room.

EXT. YARD
Lon goes slowly to sit on the iron edge of the water trough. He turns on the tap, wets his hand, pats the angry bruise on his chin.

Hud's FACE is suddenly reflected in the water.

ANOTHER ANGLE
Lon turns around to look silently at him. There is a long pause.

> HUD
> What are you lookin' at?

> LON
> I'm lookin' at you, Hud.

> HUD
> Climb off it. You've been wantin' to do pretty much the same thing. You've been wantin' to wallow her from the day she got here.

> LON
> *(quietly)*
> Yes. I've been wantin' to do it. But not mean, like you.

INT. BARN—DAY
*Lon is up in the high loft, kicking down a few dusty bales of hay to
Granddad, who is feeding the horses. They work in silence, both under a
strain. A car DRAWS UP outside.*

> LON

It's Mister Burris.

*He swings down to the ground and joins Granddad, who straightens as if to
gather his energies. Burris enters.*

> GRANDDAD

Good mornin'. You missed breakfast. Your timin's off.

> BURRIS

Thanks. I've eaten.

> GRANDDAD

Well, I guess you got something to tell us, or you wouldn't
be here.
> *(flatly)*
I guess the tests are done.

> BURRIS

Yes, sir. I'm afraid you've got the worst thing you could
have.

> GRANDDAD
> *(after a silence)*

And there's no cure at all?

> BURRIS

None we know of. It's like a bolt of lightning. It don't hurt
you till it hits, but then it hurts a lot.
> *(as Granddad remains silent)*
Your cattle are public enemies now. We gotta handle this
thing quick, before it spreads.

> GRANDDAD

What do I do? Just drive 'em in a pit and shoot 'em? I can't
abide that.

> BURRIS

I know it's a terrible thing, even to think about.

GRANDDAD

I've *seen* it, durin' the Depression, and it's a sight worse to see than it is to think about.

BURRIS

Look here, Mister Bannon. You're gettin' up in years. You can afford to slow down—the rest won't hurt your grass any. You might even sell a few oil leases.

Hud speaks dryly from behind them.

HUD

My daddy thinks oil is somethin' you stick in your salad dressin'.

GRANDDAD

If there's oil down there, you can get it sucked up after I'm under there with it. But I don't like it and I don't aim to have it. There'll be no holes punched in this land while I'm here. They ain't gonna come in and grade no roads, so the wind can blow me away.

Granddad goes to the open doorway to look out at the land sweeping away in front of him.

GRANDDAD

What's oil to me? What can I do with a bunch of ruttin' oil wells? I can't ride out every day and prowl amongst 'em, like I can my cattle. I can't breed 'em or tend 'em or rope 'em or chase 'em or nothin'. I can't feel a smidgen of pride in 'em, cause they ain't none of my doin'.

HUD
(hard)

There's money in it.

GRANDDAD
(wheeling on him)

I don't want that kinda money. I want mine to come from somethin' that keeps a man doin' for himself.

He turns and holds out his hand abruptly to Burris.

                    GRANDDAD
We're much obliged to you for comin' out in person to tell
us.

The two men shake hands.

EXT. MEADOW—DAY
*Ten bulldozers are lined up on the horizon, massive steel behemoths looking
like tanks in formation for battle. There is a deafening ROAR as they crank
up, heard all over the prairie. Clouds of dust begin to roll out over the fields
as they bite into the earth, scraping out the great pits for the slaughter.*

*Through the dust the mounted figures of Hud, Lon, and Granddad are
visible, standing motionless and watching the defacing of the land.*

EXT. PASTURE
*They begin driving the cattle, popping the reins of their bridles against their
chaps. Banks of mist rise from the dewy grass and hang gray around the
bellies of the moving cattle. In the distance the pits are waiting.*

EXT. THE PITS
*The pits are gaping holes, each with one end sloped and one end steep. The
cattle pay them little mind; they go straight down the sloped ends, curious to
see what is at the bottom.*

EXT. THE LAST PIT
*Lon stations himself, on horseback, at the slope end of the final pit. The
cattle stand quietly at the bottom, the calves sucking, the cows licking themselves and their calves. Hud steps to the edge of the pit with a clip-action rifle
in his hand. Lon is stiff in his presence, Hud abrupt.*

EXT. ANOTHER PIT
*One of the state men, BURKHART, spreads a rag on the ground and puts
several extra clips on it. Then he comes to the edge and looks down at the
cattle.*

EXT. ON A SMALL RISE
*Granddad places his horse at a vantage point where he can survey the whole
operation. He is without expression, his hands folded calmly on the saddle
horn.*

                    GRANDDAD
Start shootin'.

EXT. HUD'S PIT
The first SHOT crashes out from somewhere down the line. Lon's horse jumps and rears. Hud drops to a knee and begins shooting.

The firing of the guns and the bawling of the cattle DROWN OUT all other sound. As the guns go off Lon's horse becomes crazy with fright and he has all he can do to fight it, going around in circles, until it hangs its head and stands quivering, every muscle tight.

Not for a moment does the dust or the noise settle. All down the line the gunners kneel and fire without let-up. Hud rises, taking out his clip, going quickly to another pit. The mist, the dust, the acrid gunpowder all billow up into one huge cloud. No actual cow is seen hammered down; but that it is a welter of blood, a scene out of hell, is apparent enough from the cool, quick, methodical movements of the gunners.

Jose reels past Lon and doubles over a mesquite bush, vomiting. Lon shades his eyes in order to search out a glimpse of his grandfather.

EXT. ON THE RISE
Granddad raises a hand to point, and a gunner, following his gesture, slams out another bullet. Then the old man folds his hands on the saddle horn again.

Now the noise begins to SCATTER, just a finishing shot or two. There are SCRAPING bolts as the gunners clear their magazines. Then only the cloud and a terrible silence.

Lon spurs up to Granddad.

                    LON
Didn't take long.

                    GRANDDAD
It don't take very long to kill things. Not like it takes to grow.

He wheels his horse around savagely and gallops off. The others fall in together and troop slowly after him.

EXT. BANNON HOUSE
as the men ride in and dismount. They tie their horses and walk over to the water trough to drink.

In the background, Granddad's two longhorns are in the little feed pen, lazily pulling oat straw out of the hayrack.

THOMSON

Hey, wait a minute. We missed two of 'em. You-all stay here, I'll take care of 'em.

GRANDDAD
(a cold, even voice)

Where do you think you're goin', Mister?

THOMSON
(stopping)

To finish this job. Somebody needs to.

GRANDDAD

You just come back here. I'll kill them two myself, seein' as how I raised 'em.

Thomson seems uncertain. His hand fidgets with his gun.

GRANDDAD

Something wrong with you?

THOMSON
(mistrustfully)

There's no guarantee you'll do it.

The men stir uneasily as he calls Granddad a liar. Hud's flat voice breaks the silence.

HUD

He just said he would.

BURRIS
(to Thomson, angrily)

You get in the car. We're goin' down and finish burnin' those carcasses, and then we're leavin'.
(turns to Granddad)
Mister Bannon can take care of the rest of this without us botherin' him.

Thomson goes to the car. Burris lingers another moment, straining for something to say.

GRANDDAD

Now you go on, Mister Burris. I know this here ain't your doin'. You just see about the burnin', and then get that feller there off my ranch.

BURRIS

All I can say is I'm sorry. I'm sure sorry.

Burris turns and goes quickly. The men from the ranch watch the cars driving away.

GRANDDAD

He ain't such a bad feller. Just got a crapper of a job.

EXT. IN THE YARD
Granddad pauses a moment as he comes to Jesse and Jose.

GRANDDAD

I don't plan on havin' any work to do for some time. And I'm sorry I can't afford to keep you on till things get better. So I'll have to let you go.

Both men nod. Granddad continues across the yard, Lon still at his heels.

GRANDDAD
(to Hud)

Gimme your rifle.

Hud hands it to him. The old man hefts its weight in his hands a moment, then starts for the feed pen. Lon follows.

EXT. THE FEED PEN
Granddad leans on the fence and looks at the two old outlaw steers, the sun flashing on their sweeping horns. They raise their heads from the straw to glare at him with their wild, rolling eyes.

GRANDDAD

Lord, but I've chased them two longhorns many a mile. I don't know if I can kill 'em. But I guess I can.

Lon, a step or two behind him, is silent. The old man continues staring at the steers.

LON

I guess this is the worst thing that ever happened to you.

Granddad rubs a hand through his hair and shakes his head.

GRANDDAD

I can get over this if my health don't go to failin' me.

The longhorns lower their heads and begin snatching at the straw again.

GRANDDAD

Lon, you go away someplace.

Lon has not seen his face all this time. He nods at Granddad's back and turns to go.

EXT. SIDE OF THE BARN
as Lon comes around, out of sight of the feed pen. He finds Hud leaning against the wall, smoking in the sunshine. Lon also leans up against the wall. The two men do not look at each other.

The first SHOT crashes loudly, its echo bouncing back off the hills. Then there are three more in quick succession, and silence again.

HUD
(without expression)

Those old bulls are hard to kill.

ANOTHER ANGLE
as Granddad appears, striding toward the house, the rifle cradled across his arm, his back straight. He SHOUTS over his shoulder at Lon.

GRANDDAD

Drag 'em away and bury 'em. Bury 'em quick! Go on!

Lon jumps at the command and runs. The old man disappears into the house. Hud remains where he is, the sun on his face, smoking quietly.

INT. ALMA'S CABIN—NIGHT
She is dressed in street clothes for the first time, finishing packing. She snaps the suitcase shut, looks about the little room. Absently, she picks up a full ashtray and empties it. Then she looks at the frilly paper lampshade; she gets on a chair, pulls it off, drops it in the wastebasket. Lon appears at the door.

ALMA

Did you call about the bus for me?

LON
(nods)

It leaves at eleven-fifteen.

ALMA

Can I buy my ticket on it?

LON

Yeah, they said that'd be okay.

(pause)
Alma, I got two hundred dollars calf money, if you're short.

ALMA

You just keep it.
(she looks around the room)
Well, I'm ready.

He picks up the suitcase, politely holds the door open for her, and they go out.

EXT. THALIA GREYHOUND STATION—NIGHT
as they drive up and get out of the truck. Lon brings the suitcase and puts it down on the pavement. They face each other for the last time.

LON
Alma, I wish you weren't goin' off and leavin' us.

ALMA
You look after your grandpa. He's getting old and feeble. He's your job now.

LON
We need you around here. I sure do.

ALMA
You'll get along just fine.

LON
(painfully)
I wish you'd stay.

ALMA
I've been all over this cow country, looking for the exact right place and the exact right people, so once I got stopped I wouldn't have to be moving again. But it hasn't worked out.
(smiles at the boy)
Goodbye, honey. Take care of yourself. And don't you be lazy now.

She gives him a quick hug. He gets back into the truck and drives off.

EXT. BUS STATION
Alma remains seated as Hud approaches smoking, watching him coolly. He stands looking down at her.

HUD

Well, it looks like we're losin' a good cook.
(smiles)
Maybe we shoulda boosted your salary a little bit.
(she merely looks at him)
You're not lettin' that little ruckus we had run you off, are
you?

ALMA
(evenly)
As far as I can get on a bus ticket.

HUD

Are you claimin' I'm the first guy who ever put his foot in
your door?

ALMA

No.

HUD

But I'm the first one who ever got rough, huh?
(pauses)
Well, I'm sorry. That wasn't my style. I don't usually get
rough with my women.
(smiles again)
I generally don't have to.

ALMA

You're rough on everybody.

HUD
(unruffled)

So they tell me.

She flicks away her cigarette. As always, she is honest.

ALMA

You want to know something funny? It would have happened eventually, without the roughhouse. You look pretty
good without your shirt on, you know— the sight of that
through the kitchen window made me put my dish towel
down more 'n once.

HUD
(wryly)
Why didn't you speak up sooner?

She shrugs. The bus finally appears beside them, the door swings open. Alma rises.

HUD
I'll remember you, honey. You're the one that got away.

She gets into the bus and it goes, leaving him on the pavement.

INT. PICKUP TRUCK—MOVING SHOT
The road is empty. As usual, for company, Lon turns on his transistor radio: Wayne Rainey sings, "Why don't you haul off and love me, like you used to do? . . . "

Lon turns at the cattle guard and starts across the pasture. In his mirror he suddenly sees a pair of headlights coming up behind as fast as an ambulance. The headlights come to within a foot of his rear bumper and he sees the Cadillac grille.

INT. CADILLAC—MOVING SHOT
Hud rides the boy's tail, grinning, getting a kick out of it.

INT. PICKUP TRUCK—MOVING SHOT
Lon nervously watches his uncle's car in the mirror. When he looks back to the road again he tenses violently, slamming on the brake, swerving the wheel as hard as he can.

EXT. IN THE ROAD
Granddad is on his hands and knees, crawling, looking up into the bright LIGHTS that are rushing down on him. A quick GLIMPSE of him, no more.

In the background the horse that threw him is humping, then streaking away into the darkness.

INT. PICKUP TRUCK—MOVING SHOT
The Cadillac JARS Lon's rear end, while the boy pulls wildly on the wheel to avoid the figure in the road. He goes bouncing over the bar ditch and into the pasture, almost spinning over. There is another sudden lurch and Lon is thrown against the far door, still trying to hang on to the wheel with one hand. The truck has STOPPED, tilted over in the ditch, the music cut OFF, the night abruptly silent. Lon pounds the door open and jumps out.

EXT. IN THE ROAD
The boy runs back, looking frantically for Granddad. Hud is out in the road in front of his car. The grille of the Cadillac is caved in and Hud stands in the HEADLIGHTS slinging blood off his nose.

> HUD
>
> You stupid knuckle-head, what'd you stop for? You got your life's work ahead of you, payin' for this car!

> LON
> *(as if choking)*
>
> Didn't you see him! He's out here—Granddad. He was crawlin' in the road.

EXT. IN THE DITCH
The two men run over together. Granddad is in the ditch, still moving on his hands and knees. Hud kneels down and clasps him in his arms, trying to keep him still.

> LON
>
> Granddad, what happened?

> GRANDDAD
>
> I wanted to take a look around the place. I fell off my horse.

Hud raises his head to look at Lon.

> HUD
>
> This old man's hurt bad.

> GRANDDAD
>
> Let me up. A man ain't to crawl.

He falls silent.

> HUD
>
> Lon, take my car. Get to the house. Call an ambulance and tell 'em to get here quick. Tell 'em we got an awful sick man.

The frozen boy leaps up and runs.

INT. CADILLAC
Lon tries desperately to start it. The motor WHINES but it will not turn over. He slams the dashboard in frustration.

> LON
>
> It won't start.

HUD

All right, forget it. There's a bottle of whiskey in the dash.
Bring it over.

*Granddad lies weakly in Hud's arms, and Hud's wrists are trembling as he
holds him. Lon comes flying back with the bottle.*

HUD

Easy, easy, old man.

*He tilts Granddad's head, and Lon tries to make him take some whiskey, but
it bubbles off the old man's mouth and runs in a stream down his chin and
neck.*

GRANDDAD
(quietly)

Don't make me drink that stuff.

Lon slams the bottle on the ground.

HUD

Go on down to the main road, try to flag a car down, get
some help up here. Go on, move!

GRANDDAD

Don't send him off, Hud.

LON

I'm right here, Granddad. Don't you worry.

GRANDDAD

I feel kinda cold.

LON

You're gonna be all right.

GRANDDAD

Don't know if I want to be.

LON

Don't talk like that. You'll be just fine.

GRANDDAD

Feel like throwin' in the sponge. Feel like givin' up.

LON

You? You never quit on anything in your whole life.

> GRANDDAD
> *(evenly)*

Hud there is waitin' on me. And he ain't a patient man.

He turns his face away. There is silence.

> LON
> *(like a child)*

He isn't gone, is he?

> HUD

Yeah.

The boy touches the sleeve of the jacket.

> LON

I meant to buy him a good blanket-lined jacket, and give it to him sometime or other.

> HUD

You listen to me. I'm not lying now. It was the best thing. He was worn-out and he knew it.

> LON

But he didn't seem so bad. He didn't seem bad off at all.

> HUD

He was, Lonnie. Tryin' to get up and hurtin' himself.
> *(pauses)*

He couldn't've made it any way in the world. He couldn't've made it another hour.

Lon turns slowly away from the body and looks at Hud.

> LON

He could if he'd wanted to. You fixed it so he didn't want to anymore.

> HUD

You don't know the whole story. He and I fought many and many a round. But I guess you could say I helped him as much as he ever helped me.

> LON
> *(numb)*

How'd you help him, Hud? By tryin' to sell him out? By makin' him give up and quit? By takin' the heart out of him? Is that how you helped him?

Hud makes no defense. He just gives the boy a calm, impassive look.

EXT. CHURCH—DAY
Hud and Lon stand alone out front, where the cortege is drawn up and waiting.

> LON
> *(hotly)*

He ain't in any loaf-around eternal life. He's the way he was—enjoyin' his good horses, lookin' at the land, tryin' to figure out ways to beat the dry weather and the wind.

> HUD

Settle down, boy. We still got the graveyard ahead of us.

The doors open and the PREACHER emerges, the congregation streaming out behind him. Lon makes a move to avoid him, turning away to stand near the hearse, but the preacher approaches.

> PREACHER

I know what you're feeling, but look at it this way. He's gone to a better place, my boy.

> LON

I don't think so. Not unless dirt is a better place than air.

Lon turns away from them all and walks quickly down the street, going alone.

EXT. RANCH—DAY
Hud pulls up in his Cadillac and finds Lon surveying the land.

> HUD
> *(quietly)*

Well, we took him to the graveyard and put him down. It's all over with now.

The boy says nothing. He picks up a plain brown paper bag. Hud pulls the car around to follow him as he walks.

HUD

What've you got there?

LON

My gear.

HUD

You goin' someplace?

LON

Yeah.

HUD

You're travelin' pretty light.

LON

I got everything I need.

HUD

Plannin' to go for good?

LON

That's right.

Hud finds that he has come up against something new in Lon.

HUD

What about your half of this spread?

LON

You can put my share in the bank. I'm going somewhere
else and work a while, if I can happen onto a job.

HUD

Aren't you a little bit green to go bustin' loose on your
own?

LON

Well, we'll see.

Hud is silent a moment.

HUD
(with faint mockery)

I was just about your age when I went off to the army. Your
granddaddy bought me a Mars candy bar down at the station, and he said to me, "Character's the only thing I've got
to give you. Be a man."

> LON
> *(evenly)*

I suppose he was kinda worried—you tryin' so hard to get out of the draft and all.

> HUD

Honcho.

> *(the boy stops)*

I just want you to know that if you don't make your million, you can always come back and work for me.

> LON

I won't be back this way.

> HUD
> *(good-humored)*

I guess you've come to be of your granddaddy's opinion—that I ain't fit to live with.

> *(the boy is silent)*

Too bad. We might've whooped it up a little bit, you and me. That's the way you used to want it.

> LON

I used to. So long, Hud.

> HUD

You know something, fantan? This world is so full of crap, a man's gonna get into it sooner or later, whether he's careful or not.

Lon goes, walking down the dirt road that leads to the highway. Hud watches him.

The bend in the road takes the boy out of sight after a moment. Hud looks slowly around. There is a sense of things finished and at an end here. The yard is empty, the corral is empty, the cabin is empty, the bunkhouse is empty. Hud is alone.

> **THE END**

Norma Rae

Produced by Tamara Asseyev and Alex Rose, *Norma Rae* was released by Twentieth Century Fox in 1979. Its cast included:

Norma Rae .... Sally Field
Sonny .... Beau Bridges
Reuben .... Ron Leibman
Vernon .... Pat Hingle
Leona .... Barbara Baxley
Bonnie Mae .... Gail Strickland
Wayne Billings .... Morgan Paull
Ellis Harper .... John Calvin
Dr. Watson .... Booth Colman
Reverend Hubbard .... Vernon Weddle

FADE IN:

UNDER TITLES

SERIES OF PHOTOGRAPHS
They succeed one another with the SOUND of a CAMERA CLICKING sharply.

This is a composite of NORMA RAE WEBSTER's life, glimpses of her early days, a burgeoning and a metamorphosis:

She is seen as an infant, sitting in her bath in a galvanized tub, hair twisted into a kewpie-doll peak, beribboned.

Norma at seven, front tooth out, a large grin splitting her face.

At twelve in a bathing suit, a pigeon-toed stance, arms folded self-consciously across her chest.

At fifteen, facing front, arrogant now, breasts jutting out, hip cocked.

At eighteen, her arm around a sailor's shoulder, wearing his hat at a rakish angle.

At twenty, on a front porch with a cluster of girls, Norma at the center, mouth black with too much lipstick, holding a ukulele.

At twenty-two, holding a bridal bouquet, wearing a floppy hat, perplexed, faintly forlorn, on the edge of the unknown.

At twenty-four, defiant, thumbing her nose at a sign reading "Simpson's Secretarial School."

At twenty-six, sitting with her back against a tree, two young children tumbled in her lap, looking fond and frazzled.

191

At twenty-eight, in a monkey-pert waitress's outfit, balancing a tray, ground lost.

At thirty, a photographer's formal portrait, unguarded, beautiful, unfathomable.

At thirty-two, mature, strong, with humor, without illusion.

NORMA
She moves—and the photograph becomes film.

CAMERA PULLS BACK.
In the noise, amid the flying lint, she is in an aisle tight with machines, monitoring looms.

THE MILL
The place bursts on the SCREEN like a battlefield, full of a jolting, nerve-shattering din. In the enormous space, rows and rows of old WOODEN LOOMS ROAR like waterfalls and shake the floors with ceaseless trembling vibrations. The sound is deafening, the constant, punishing, racketing motion disorienting. There are no windows, no sunlight, only blank, brick walls; it is a seasonless, timeless world in which men and women cannot hear themselves think, do not think. They are bound and shackled to the work.

Steam vents spew mist into every corner to keep the yarn hot and wet. Mosquito netting rises from the floor and disappears overhead in the high dark reaches toward the ceiling. There is a permanent haze everywhere made by lint coming off the rolls of terry cloth, rolls as high as a man.

ANOTHER ANGLE
The work begins in "the raw" where the cotton bales are brought in and men with surgical masks covering their noses and mouths rip apart the bales of cotton, feeding them into the mouths of hoppers that shred the cotton fibers and rip them apart.

Cotton dust and lint fill the air like snow, coating everyone from head to foot.

ANOTHER ANGLE
Carders are next on the line, then spinners and doffers. Almost all the work can be seen in this vast room, the size of an enormous pasture, without interior walls. The rolls of terry cloth slowly unwind behind the backs of the side hemmers, passing yard by yard through the women's sewing machines.

LEONA WITCHARD
gray-streaked, traces of beauty still visible. She works with her face close to a spider web of threads, her hands rapidly guiding them. It is work of intense concentration, demanding, exhausting.

VERNON WITCHARD
Norma's father, a large, handsome man, fractious, expansive, stands at a row of bobbins, doing back-breaking stoop labor.

A shrill WHISTLE SOUNDS. It is the break for lunch.

Vernon Witchard straightens, clutching his back, punished by the morning's work.

INT. LUNCHROOM
A narrow space with a long window looking out on the work floor. Signs are posted: "Give your chair to a spinner—they only have 15 minutes." The mill hands make quick work of their meal. There is little conversation; they are already too tired to talk.

Norma munches on an apple. BONNIE MAE, a cheerful sparrow of a woman from the folding tables, speaks to her.

> **BONNIE MAE**
> You just eating an apple for lunch?

> **NORMA**
> I'm dieting.

> **BONNIE MAE**
> Well, I gotta keep my strength up.
> *(eats heartily, biting into a thick sandwich)*
> I put this jelly up myself. On Sunday, Roscoe and I put up over sixty quarts of peaches. What'd you do over the weekend, Norma?

> **NORMA**
> Soaked my feet.

> **BONNIE MAE**
> Saw you downtown. Your friend drives a big car.

> **NORMA**
> If you'd looked on the motel register, you'd a seen my name there, too.

> **BONNIE MAE**
> It's none of my business . . .

Norma turns to look at her mother beside her. The woman's eyes are closed, her head rests back against the tile.

NORMA
Momma, you haven't opened your sack.

Leona remains motionless.

NORMA
Momma, don't you want your lunch?

Still the woman doesn't answer.

NORMA
Momma!

Still Leona remains with her eyes closed. Alarmed, Norma shakes her and Leona finally opens her eyes, looking at her daughter blankly.

NORMA
What is it, Momma? Don't you feel good?

LEONA
What?

NORMA
Don't you hear me? *Momma!*
(bends close to her, bawling)
Momma, Momma, Momma!

Leona doesn't respond. Norma is on her feet, instantly. She hauls her mother up, grabs her by the arm, and, pulling her, she runs.

THE WEAVING ROOM
It is a headlong race across the length of the mill, Norma ahead and frantic, her mother in tow.

INT. DOCTOR'S OFFICE
DR. WATSON is confronted by an agitated, flaring Norma, while Leona sits with her hands calmly folded in her lap.

NORMA
She didn't hear me! She didn't hear one word I said! She doesn't hear you now!

DR. WATSON
You know this happens, Norma Rae. It happens all the time.

NORMA
Well, not to my momma!

DR. WATSON
It'll pass off. It's just temporary.

NORMA
That makes it all right, huh? She's only deaf for an hour,
she's only deaf for two hours, she's only deaf all *day*!

DR. WATSON
(mildly)
She can get herself another job.

NORMA
What other job in this town? This is the *only* job.

DR. WATSON
I'll give her a note. They'll send her home.

NORMA
(bitterly)
Come on, Momma. You're nothing to any of 'em.

She takes her mother's arm and shepherds her out.

EXT. THE YARD OF THE WITCHARD HOUSE
*The back of the shotgun house sits in a small, grassy plot. In one corner of the
yard a shade tree struggles to live. It is still daylight, and underneath,
standing by a table, Leona Witchard transfers small plants from ponies into
pots.*

INT. KITCHEN
*Norma is at the sink, washing the dishes; her father Vernon, towel in hand,
dries. Norma, as she works, watches her mother through the open window.
She finally calls out to her.*

NORMA
You all right out there?

Without turning, Leona responds in her quiet, patient voice.

LEONA
Yes. I'm all right.

NORMA
You'll get all bitten up.

LEONA
I'm coming in soon.

Norma returns to the job at hand. She suddenly wipes her hands briskly on a towel.

> NORMA
> I'm gonna let this pot soak.

> VERNON
> *(mildly)*
> There's one soaking from breakfast.

> NORMA
> Well, now it's got company.

She goes out.

INT. LIVING ROOM
In the sparsely furnished room, two children, CRAIG and MILLIE, sit raptly watching TELEVISION. Norma enters.

> NORMA
> Ten more minutes of that junk and then you do your homework.

> CRAIG
> I did it.

> NORMA
> "C" in writing, "C" in spelling, "D" in reading—you haven't been doing too much homework.

> MILLIE
> Sssshhh. I wanna hear.

> NORMA
> I'll ssshhh you.

She goes into her bedroom, strips off her blouse, sniffs the armpits, grimaces and tosses it aside. She takes one from the closet and puts it on.

WIDER ANGLE
as Vernon looms in the doorway.

> VERNON
> What're you getting fixed up for?

> NORMA
> I'm going into town.

> VERNON

What do you need in town?

> NORMA

Things.

> VERNON

Well . . . I'll drive you in.

> NORMA

You got "Bonanza" on next.

> VERNON

I'll miss it. Same every week anyhow.

> NORMA

I'm going to J.C. Penney's to buy myself some panties and a white cotton brassiere, size 32C. You wanna come sit on a little stool outside the dressing room and have all the ladies look at you, come on.

> VERNON

Well, I don't think I care to do that . . .
> *(then)*
You comin' straight back?

> NORMA

No. Next I'm going to the drugstore to buy myself some Kotex pads and a *Cosmopolitan* magazine.

> VERNON

Well . . . *then* you coming home?

> NORMA

Yeah. By then I'll be so tired out from all the excitement, I'll be coming home.

The DOORBELL RINGS. Vernon goes to answer it.

ANGLE ON THE FRONT DOOR
REUBEN WARSHOVSKY stands on the stoop. He is dressed in tennis shoes, blue jeans and a T-shirt. Reuben is lean, sharp, full of nervous and intellectual energy; his view of life wavers between the jaundiced and the merry. He is a master of finagle and accommodation; he is purposeful and principled. He is fully mobilized always, however calm and easy his manner may be.

REUBEN

Mr. Witchard?

VERNON

That's right. Vernon Witchard. Who're you?

REUBEN

My name is Reuben Warshovsky.

VERNON

Warshovsky? What kind of name is that?

REUBEN

It's the kind you have to spell for telephone operators and headwaiters.

VERNON

What do you want?

REUBEN

I'd like to get me a room with a mill family.

VERNON

What for? We got a hotel with 12 rooms and a motel with 36 rooms.

REUBEN

I want to get to know some mill hands. Close up.

VERNON

Why is that?

REUBEN

Mr. Witchard . . . I got into town about an hour ago, parked my rented car, got out, and, before I could adjust my crotch, the chief of police was on me, saying, "Who are you, I don't know you" and "what the hell are you doing here?" I told him I was a labor organizer, come to put a union in the O.P. Henley textile mill, and he said, "The fuck you are!" gave me a ticket, and told me to get my ass elsewhere right quick.

Norma has appeared behind her father and listens curiously.

VERNON

He's dead right. As far as I'm concerned, you're all communists or agitators or crooks or Jews or all four together.

Any town you show up, folks get thrown out of work and get their heads busted.

REUBEN

What do you make an hour, Mr. Witchard?

VERNON

I make a dollar and thirty-five cents a frame.

REUBEN

When did you have your last cost-of-living raise?

VERNON

I never had that.

REUBEN

With all due respect, Mr. Witchard, with today's inflation, that makes you a shlemiel.

VERNON

You calling me some kind of name or other?

REUBEN

You're underpaid. You're overworked. They're shafting you, right up to your tonsils. You need me.

VERNON

If you hurry, you can get to the fence before my dog bites you.

NORMA

What're you telling him that for? We don't have a dog.

REUBEN
(looking at her father)

You don't need one.

INT. GOLDEN CHERRY MOTEL

The place has never seen better days. It was always none too clean, familiar with the hot-pillow trade and other transients. The rooms have a view of a blacktop parking area and a scummy swimming pool.

Norma sits in the small lobby, flipping through the pages of a magazine, ignored by ALSTON PURVIS, the desk clerk. She looks up with some surprise as Reuben enters, by now footsore. He recognizes her.

                    REUBEN
This is one friendly little town you got here. I've been told
to shove off, to piss off, and to git off.

                    NORMA
                    (mildly)
This place is okay. Just make sure they spray the room for
roaches.

                    REUBEN
I'm familiar with roaches.
                    (goes to the desk)
I'd like a room with a view.

                    ALSTON
You got the back alley or the parking lot. Which?

                    REUBEN
                    (to Norma)
Back alley or parking lot?

                    NORMA
                    (intervening)
Give him 31, Alston. You can't hear the drunks in there.

*GEORGE BENSON enters. He is a large man, floridly handsome, com-
manding, with an edge of violence just concealed. He walks straight past
Norma for the stairs, making only a peremptory beckoning gesture. She
tosses aside the magazine and rises to follow.*

INT. MOTEL ROOM
*The SHOWER is HEARD RUNNING from the open bathroom. Norma sits
on the edge of the torn-apart bed, fastening her bra; she gets up and pulls on
her jeans. Her face is impassive; whatever has transpired in the past hour has
left her unmoved.*

*George comes in, a towel wrapped around his middle, his hair still stream-
ing. He combs his hair at the mirror, drops of water spraying.*

                    GEORGE
I'll be back this way next Wednesday. After dinner. I'm
having dinner with my wife's folks.

                    NORMA
Tonight was the last time, George.

He doesn't turn. The comb simply moves a little more slowly.

GEORGE

You don't say, Norma Rae. Isn't that a surprising turn.

NORMA

No. It's been coming for some time.

GEORGE

Well, isn't that funny, I didn't notice it. Didn't you get your steak dinner? Didn't you get your box of pralines? Didn't you come three times in a row in that bed over there?

NORMA

I wasn't counting.

GEORGE
(now turns to face her)
Looks like I don't know what it takes to satisfy you these days.

NORMA

It just doesn't sit well with me anymore, George. You got your wife, you got your two kids in high school, there's a lot of gossip, I got *my* two kids . . .
(shrugs)
. . . I don't know . . . It just doesn't make me feel good.

GEORGE
(flatly)
You're here to make *me* feel good.

He advances on her.

NORMA

I'm not trotting down here anymore.

GEORGE

Why, you hick. You got dirt under your fingernails, you leave hair in the sink, you pick your teeth with a matchbook—I've seen you! Why, shit, what are you good for—to come out of the factory, wash under your armpits, spread your legs for a poke, and go home. And you're dumping *me!*

He hits her hard across the mouth; the impact sends her hurtling across the room, slamming against the opposite wall.

WALKWAY
She stumbles once or twice in the walkway, pauses to shove her blouse inside her pants.

Reuben is standing at the open door to his room as she passes it. He speaks coolly.

> REUBEN
> I heard a hell of a thump.

> NORMA
> That was me, getting thrown across the room.

> REUBEN
> I've got some ice for that. Come on in.

She follows him into his room.

INT. REUBEN'S ROOM
He goes into the bathroom, returns with a washcloth, dumps ice cubes out of his coke, hands her the icepack. She puts it gingerly against her face.

> REUBEN
> Sit down. You look a little shaken up.

She sits. He notes the condition she's in.

> REUBEN
> I thought everyone down South was Ashley Wilkes.

> NORMA
> You lie down with dogs, you get fleas.
> *(removes rag and shows him her nose)*
> Does this look like it's broken to you?

> REUBEN
> No, I don't think so. Want an aspirin?

> NORMA
> No, thanks.

> REUBEN
> Band-Aid?

> NORMA
> No.

> REUBEN
> Valium?

NORMA
You're a whole drugstore.

REUBEN
Mild hypochondriac. Keep the ice on it.

NORMA
Me and men. I ought to learn to say No from the start. But if it wasn't men, I don't know what it would be.

ANOTHER ANGLE
She gets up and begins to wander around. He has already established himself; books are stacked and piled everywhere, papers litter the desk, clothes are dumped on the bed and hanging from the backs of chairs.

NORMA
You got a lot of books.

REUBEN
Yeah, I'm afraid I'll wake up in a motel room someday with nothing to read but the phone book.

She stops at the picture of a girl that has been propped up on the bureau. She studies it.

NORMA
She's got big eyes.

REUBEN
She's also got a big brain.

NORMA
What's her name?

REUBEN
Dorothy Finkelstein. She's a hotshot labor lawyer out of Harvard.

NORMA
She must be your girl friend if you haul her picture around with you.

REUBEN
Well, we sleep together on Sunday mornings and then we read the *New York Times*. I guess that makes her my girl friend.

                    NORMA
                        (holds out her hand)
I'm Norma Rae Wilson.

                    REUBEN
                        (shaking)
Reuben Warshovsky.

                    NORMA
Pleased to meet you.

                    REUBEN
My pleasure.

                    NORMA
                        (pauses)
I'm sorry about my daddy. He's got a short fuse.

                    REUBEN
My credentials keep me out of a lot of places. But every
once in a while, somebody'll open a door and put me in the
best bedroom and treat me like I was a cousin.

                    NORMA
That sure as heck wouldn't be my daddy.
                        (then, abruptly)
You a Jew?

                    REUBEN
I beg your pardon?

                    NORMA
Are you a Jew?

                    REUBEN
Born and bred.

                    NORMA
I never met a Jew before. I heard they had horns.

                    REUBEN
Circumcised, yes. Horns, no.

                    NORMA
Far as I can see, you don't look any different from us.

REUBEN
We are.

NORMA
Yeah? What makes you different?

REUBEN
History.

NORMA
Oh.

She looks at him thoughtfully a moment. He is a strange bird.

NORMA
Well, thanks for the ice.

She hands back the washcloth.

REUBEN
Any time.

NORMA
Christ, I hope not.

She goes out.

EXT. MILL
Norma and her parents and a throng of mill workers surge through the chain link fence toward the looming, dirt-streaked, windowless red brick building which will swallow them all for the day. It is a spiritless mass of people, silently set for their labor, carrying with them the weariness of season after season. There are no swapped greetings; this work exacts a toll in mind and muscle.

REUBEN
(repeats over and over as he hands out leaflets)
Good morning . . . I'm from the Textile Workers' Union of America . . . Read this when you have a chance . . . Good morning . . .

NORMA AND REUBEN
As she goes through the fence, she comes face to face with Reuben again; his energy is up. He thrusts a leaflet from a large stack under his arm at each man and woman who pass. Suddenly, he finds he is handing one to Norma. She scans it quickly.

NORMA

There's too many big words in here. If I don't understand it, they ain't gonna understand it.

She shoves it back at him and is immediately lost in the crowd. He stops his activity and stands there in some puzzlement, reading his own flyer once again.

NORMA
A bossman, JIMMY JEROME DAVIS, stands in front of her as she is about to enter the building.

JIMMY

That fellow a friend of yours, Norma?

NORMA
(shrugging)

Looks like he's getting to be.

JIMMY

Better hotfoot it or you'll be late.

NORMA

I don't care if I don't get there till tomorrow.

But she goes in.

AT THE FENCE
The last of the mill hands has entered. Reuben is finally alone and prepares to go. But as he turns, he finds Jimmy Jerome in his path.

JIMMY

Well . . . one of you guys shows up about every four years— about the same time we get the locusts.

REUBEN
(flat)

What's your name?

JIMMY

My name? My name's Jimmy Jerome Davis.

REUBEN

Well, Jimmy Jerome, we already got six of you bossmen in civil contempt. Maybe we can make it seven.

JIMMY
(genial)
Why, hell, we plaster the toilet with them things.

He turns and goes. The gate in the fence closes and Reuben is on the outside.

NORMA
in the weaving room, the back of her shirt already wet.

TEDDY BOB KELLER, a fellow worker, taps her on the shoulder; she looks around; he indicates a BOSSMAN beckoning to her from his office.

NORMA
I already told him I wouldn't go out to dinner with him. What's he want now?

TEDDY BOB
Maybe he wants to make it breakfast, Norma Rae.

She makes a deprecating gesture and marches off to the summons.

INT. OFFICE
It is quiet in here behind the large plate glass window through which the entire activity in the weaving room can be surveyed. TOMMY GARDNER waits for Norma behind a desk. He has the hard look of a hard-living man, used to dealing with hunting dogs and menials. Norma enters and goes on the attack.

NORMA
Whatever it is, I didn't do it.

GARDNER
Norma, you got the biggest mouth in this mill. Give us longer breaks, give us more smoking time, give us a Kotex machine—

NORMA
Do it and I'll shut up.

GARDNER
Well, we're gonna do better'n that. We figure the only way to close that mouth is to hand you a promotion. You're rising in the world, honey.

NORMA
Yeah? How far and for how much?

> ### GARDNER
> We're gonna put you on as a spot-checker.

> ### NORMA
> It ain't gonna make me any friends.

> ### GARDNER
> It's gonna make you another dollar and a half an hour.

She chews it over. It seems hard to digest.

NORMA
She is on the floor, clipboard in one hand, stopwatch in the other. She has paused behind LUCIUS WHITE, a black man, and is timing him as he rethreads a loom. When he finishes, she clicks her watch, enters a notation on the board, moves on.

ANOTHER ANGLE
She is behind GEORGE HUBBARD, watches as he unstops a spindle. Again, she clicks her watch, marks his time.

ANOTHER ANGLE
She times RAY BUCK completing a run of towels, records his speed.

ANOTHER ANGLE
Finally, she stands behind her father. Vernon works at the bobbins, doing the job he has done all his life. He pauses only an instant to rub the back of his neck, hurries to recover the tempo. He grins at his daughter over his shoulder.

Norma is troubled and unhappy.

> ### VERNON
> How'm I doin', little girl?

> ### NORMA
> You better speed it up, Daddy—if you can.

> ### VERNON
> *(protesting)*
> I'm goin' as fast as I can.

> ### NORMA
> They're watching me and they're watching you . . .

The old man grimly bends forward and his hands fly as he pulls bobbins and threads them.

EXT. VERNON'S YARD
Vernon stands on the open back porch at a galvanized tub, scrubbing his hands and face. As he dries off, he uses the towel to whack some of the clinging lint from his shirt and his pants.

Norma comes out on the porch; she goes to brush the lint that mats his hair, making him look like a white-haired man of eighty. Vernon stiffly pulls away from her.

NORMA
Well, I suppose you're sore at me.

VERNON
I don't think you should push your own daddy.

NORMA
(wrestles with it)
It's more money. I need it for my kids.

VERNON
Well, I don't need it from *my* kid.

And he walks into the house, his back stiff.

Norma stands troubled. She calls out to her children, almost absently.

NORMA
Craig . . . Millie . . . get out of Grandma's marigolds.

EXT. BASEBALL FIELD—NIGHT
A game is in progress on the pokey little baseball diamond with weak night lights and splintered, faded green, two-tiered set of bleachers. Bugs wheel endlessly around the lights; tree FROGS CROAK; there is nothing so grand as uniforms—the two teams play in their work clothes. The scoreboard, broken and sagging, reads: "MILLAGEVILLE 15, PISTON 12."

There is a sudden thunderclap of wild excitement, bringing everyone to their feet, as the batter powers one far into the darkness of right field, bringing in the two men already on base and tying the score.

IN THE STANDS
Norma Rae and Bonnie Mae sit down again with flushed faces.

NORMA
Want something?

BONNIE MAE

Bring me a hot dog, lotsa relish.

Norma climbs over some people and goes down the steps.

BEHIND THE STANDS

A hot dog wagon steams; the bugs have concentrated here as well. Norma runs into Reuben at the counter, slathering mustard and relish on his dog.

NORMA
(to the vendor)

Two dogs, lotsa relish and no relish.

She turns to Reuben.

NORMA

Enjoying the game?

REUBEN

I like that shortstop. He goes into the hole.

NORMA

That's J.C. McAllister. Scouts've been looking at him.

Reuben takes a first big bite out of his hot dog and instantly spits it out, spraying dog and bun everywhere.

NORMA

What's the matter? Don't you like it?

REUBEN

Well, it's not Nathan's. In fact, I'm not even sure it's a hot dog.
(he chucks the remainder away in a trash barrel)
What do they put in these things?

NORMA

A lot of red dye—and other things you don't want to know about.

The CROWD YELLS. Apparently, something interesting has happened.

ANOTHER ANGLE

ELLIS HARPER comes up to the wagon. He is tall, good-looking, fine-boned, educated. When he sees Norma, he stops; there is a sense of constraint between them.

ELLIS

Hello, Norma.

NORMA

Hello, Ellis.

ELLIS

You're looking fine.

NORMA

I'm always fine. I'm a horse.

ELLIS

You changed your hair.

NORMA

It grew.

ELLIS
(after a moment's silence)

How's Craig?

NORMA

He lost a tooth . . .
(voice flattens)
. . . It wouldn't hurt if you came by to see him once in a while.

ELLIS

I don't think I should do that, Norma.

NORMA

Suit yourself—you always have.

The man stands uncomfortably a moment, then quickly turns and walks away.

Reuben plunks down a few coins on the counter.

REUBEN

I'll have an RC Cola.
(then to her)
Want one?

NORMA

Yeah.

> REUBEN
> *(with additional coins)*

Make it two.

MOVING SHOT

Drinks in hand, they wander around the perimeter of the ball field. Cars are parked facing the game, spectators sitting in them, drinking beer; kids sit or lie atop sedans, watching the action.

Young kids on bikes stand, one foot on the pedal, one on the ground. A few young couples sit in the grass, infants crawling not too far from them.

As usual, Norma says what she is thinking, without preamble, out loud, directly.

> NORMA

I climbed in the backseat of his Cadillac on a rainy night six years ago, stuck my feet out the window, and got me my little Craig off that southern gentleman.
> *(dismissively)*
He's never done anything worthwhile since.

> REUBEN

Were you married?

> NORMA

He didn't bother and I didn't bother.

> REUBEN

My first affair, as I recollect it, was with my Hungarian piano teacher. I was playing Smetana and she put her head in my lap. I played the hell out of it. We ended up in the bedroom under a Russian icon, and her husband came home and found us and burst into tears. I went and put my arms around him and said, "I'm sorry, I'm sorry," and then we all went into the kitchen and had a glass of tea.

She looks at him oddly.

> NORMA

Seems like every time you run into me, I'm hassling with some other guy.

> REUBEN

That's what it seems like.

NORMA
What do you think of me, I wonder?

REUBEN
I think you're too smart for what's happening to you.

He lets her think that over—and she does. They keep walking in silence.

INT. THE ROVING ROOM
Norma, with clipboard and stopwatch, makes her rounds. She stops to time SONNY WEBSTER, an intense, hidden, unfathomable young man; the surface is calm but frustration is just beneath it. As she clicks her watch to start, he does an extraordinary thing—he leaps away from the loom, runs to another, starts it, calls to her over his shoulder, taunting her:

SONNY
Come on, lady! I'm over here now!

MOVING SHOT
She starts to follow him, bewildered; he darts to a third loom.

SONNY
I'm right over here now! I got the jump on you now!

He weaves in and out among the looms, calling, mocking her with a crazy challenge.

SONNY
I'm behind you now. Yoo-hoo, lady! Why don't you clock me over here? I'm over here now!

ANOTHER ANGLE
She pelts after him at a dead run, finally grabbing him by the arm, stopping him.

NORMA
You damn fool, you're gonna get us both to lose our jobs!

He pulls free and rushes to yet another loom and gets it going. Norma stops, throwing up her hands.

INT. WITCHARD LIVING ROOM
Vernon has the children on his lap, watching the TELEVISION screen. Leona is across from him in a splint chair, sewing.

The DOORBELL RINGS.

NORMA

I'll get it.

She goes through the room toward the door.

AT THE DOOR
Sonny Webster is there when she opens it. She closes it in his face immediately. Then, bethinking herself, she slowly opens it again.

Sonny is quite different now, subdued, chastened.

SONNY

I won't trouble you. I just came to apologize. I know I could've lost you your job today.

NORMA

You sure went crazy on me.

SONNY

I know. I got handed divorce papers this morning. I guess I went off my head.

NORMA

Things can get to you.

SONNY

Would you come and have a drink with me, to make up for the ruckus and all the bother I put you to?

She hesitates a moment, considering it.

SONNY

I'm Sonny Webster. You used to come in my momma's bakery.

NORMA

Yeah, I remember you now, on the cash register after school. You never made the right change.

SONNY

I never did too good in math.

NORMA
(ruminating)

Sonny Webster . . .

SONNY

How about that drink?

NORMA

Okay. Wait here.

IN THE HALL

She closes the door on him, goes to get her purse and a sweater off a hook in the hall. Her father is right at her heels.

VERNON

Who's that? I heard a man's voice.

NORMA

Yeah, you did, and I'm going out with him.

VERNON

Where'd you meet him?

NORMA

Just now on the front porch!

VERNON

Some Tom, Dick, or Harry comes to the door and you got your hat on? *No,* sir!

NORMA

I'm over twenty-one—*way* over.

VERNON

Lemme say some names to you, Norma. Buddy Wilson, Ellis Harper, George Benson, a U.S. sailor, a Trailways bus driver—none of which is lookin' after you, as far as I can see. I got that spot. It's *my* food, it's *my* roof.

NORMA

There's something wrong with all this. Something wrong with the way you try to keep men off me.

VERNON

There is nothing wrong with a daddy's love for his little girl. You oughta be grateful for your daddy's love.

NORMA

You're loving me to death.

She slams out of the house.

INT. A TAVERN
Men lined at the bar still grimy from the job, getting the taste of work out of their mouths; drink ends almost every day and it is not boisterous—it is serious and dogged, an anodyne.

At the back, Norma and Sonny sit in a wooden booth, marked with cigarette burns. Soft drinks, a bucket of ice, and a bottle of bourbon in a brown paper bag stand on the scarred linoleum-topped table; they have made considerable inroads in the liquor.

A Dolly Parton RECORD is PLAYING on the JUKEBOX.

> NORMA

That woman sure can sing . . . and those words are true, too.

> SONNY

I liked Elvis, myself . . .

> NORMA
> *(high)*

I'd like to get rich by just opening my mouth and wailing . . .

> SONNY

It don't necessarily make them happy.

> NORMA
> *(the philosopher)*

What does, what does, what does?

> SONNY

A man and a woman is about your best chance.

> NORMA

You're a fine one to talk. Didn't you tell me you took a gun, went slinking along on your belly in the bushes, drew a bead on your wife, aiming to blow her head off?

> SONNY

Yeah, I was gonna burn 'em both down . . . her and her boyfriend . . . but I couldn't . . .
> *(pauses)*

She was a good person when we went together in school and all. She was a real nice person . . . but the change that come about in her . . . it still really amazes me . . .

NORMA
Listen, I'm different than what I was, too. You go through things.

She tips herself another consoling glassful. In the process, she looks up and sees someone.

REUBEN
He is at the bar, turned on the stool face to face with ORA PURSLEY, in close conference, exhorting him, proselytizing.

ANOTHER ANGLE
Norma waves at him from the booth.

NORMA
Hey! You! New York!

Reuben, a bit startled, turns and sees her.

NORMA
(gesture is expansive)
Come on over. Sit with us.

SONNY
(thwarted)
Do we need anybody else?

NORMA
(high)
The more, the merrier.

AT THE BOOTH
as Reuben approaches and stands at the booth.

NORMA
Reuben, this is Sonny. Sonny, that's Reuben.

The two men shake hands.

NORMA
Get off your feet. What are you doing here?

REUBEN
Working.

NORMA
This is a drinking place.

REUBEN

Drunk or sober, I want 'em.

SONNY

Can I pour you out one?

He brandishes the paper bag.

REUBEN

I'll have some plain seltzer.

SONNY

You just drinking soda water?

REUBEN

That's all.

Sonny pours him a glass.

SONNY

You'll feel better'n I will tomorrow morning.

NORMA

Reuben's a union man. Thinks he can put a union in the mill.

SONNY

Ain't ever been one.

REUBEN

Then its hour's come, hasn't it?

SONNY

There better be more'n one of you. 'Cause there's more'n one of them.

REUBEN

There will be.

SONNY

These big companies get everything they want. Everything goes to the rich man.

REUBEN

Getting tired of it?

SONNY

When I do, I just wash it down with beer . . .

He drinks. A boozy melancholy enfolds them, heightened by a ballad sung by Johnny Cash on the JUKEBOX. It plunges Norma into deeper gloom.

NORMA
That record was playing on the record player the night they called me up to tell me my husband was killed in a fight in a beer joint.

SONNY
I knew Buddy Wilson in high school. We had wood shop together.

NORMA
He got drunk and broke a beer bottle and got into a fight. Somebody else had a broken beer bottle, too . . . I remember going to the funeral home. This man comes to the door. I wanted to go in and see Buddy but he said he didn't have him prepared, and he didn't think it would be a good idea for me to see him. I really wanted to see him, but Daddy wouldn't let me go in . . .
(shrugs)
And that was the end of Buddy, as far as that goes . . .

ON THE STREET
The three have come out on the deserted sidewalk. The tavern lights go off behind them. Norma and Sonny are carrying a full load.

NORMA
I'm gonna drive.

SONNY
No, I'll drive.

NORMA
You're drunk.

SONNY
So're you.

REUBEN
I'll drive.

He herds them toward his car.

MOVING SHOT—CAR
Reuben is at the wheel, Norma in the middle, Sonny on the side.

NORMA

Well, I went out with one man and I'm coming home with two. That oughta surprise my daddy some.

SONNY

He sure watches you close.

NORMA

We *are* close. He used to drive 250 miles to Crescent Beach to buy me a chicken dinner, take me swimming, tell me jokes. We'd sleep in the back of the car parked on the beach and walk on the sand in the morning.
(waggles her fingers)
He bought me this ring on my finger . . .

She suddenly turns to address Reuben politely.

NORMA

Could you stop the car? I'm gonna be sick.

Reuben pulls over and stops instantly, getting out and helping her out the door.

SONNY
(apologetically, helpless)
I can't help, Norma, or I'd give it up, too.

BY THE SIDE OF THE ROAD
Norma is crouched in the bushes, Reuben bent over her, holding her waist with one hand, her forehead with the other.

She straightens at last, wan but recovered.

NORMA

Well, that's real ladylike of me . . .

REUBEN

Don't worry. I did bedpans one summer at Stuyvesant Hospital.

NORMA

One of these days I'm gonna put myself all together.

REUBEN

Make it soon. Because one of these days, I'm going to start in on you.

Her look says it can't be now. He helps her back to the car.

FRONT OF THE MILL
Another work day, the mill hands streaming through the gate. Reuben is once again stationed at his post, handing out leaflets.

Norma falls behind her father and mother to take one from him. She reads it.

> REUBEN
> I took your advice. I'm down to two syllables.

> NORMA
> One's better.

She hands it back to him and goes jauntily into the mill.

ON THE FLOOR
As she enters the tremendous weaving room floor, stopwatch and clipboard at the ready, she comes face to face with LUCIUS GREENE and gives him a cheery greeting.

> NORMA
> Hi, Lucius.

Lucius gives her a long, cold look, then deliberately turns his back. Norma stares after him, surprised, then turns and goes on.

ANOTHER ANGLE
LINETTE ODUM is heading for the looms. Norma hails her.

> NORMA
> 'Morning, Linette.

The woman deliberately stops, looks her up and down, head to toe, and then without a word moves to her place.

ANOTHER ANGLE
Norma, disturbed now, goes up to BILLY JOE STETTIN and taps him on the shoulder.

> NORMA
> Hiya, Billy Joe.

The man doesn't answer.

> NORMA
> What the hell is going on around here? I'm talking to you!

Billy Joe turns to her and spits out one word.

BILLY JOE

Fink.

NORMA

Well, shit!

And without a pause she wheels around and marches toward Tommy Gardner's office.

INT. OFFICE
She bangs open the door and, without ceremony, bursts in. Gardner looks up from his desk.

NORMA
Nobody out there's talking to me!

GARDNER
Less talk, more work.

NORMA
They're my friends and they're gonna stay my friends! I'm quitting! I'm quitting right here, I'm quitting right now. You're speeding 'em up and then you're gonna weed 'em out!

GARDNER
You knew all that.

NORMA
Well, I was greedy and I was dumb and now I'm *sorry*. You can fire me!

GARDNER
No, we won't do that. We'll just put you back in the weaving room, Norma. Your family's been in this mill for a long time.

She plunks the instruments of her now-hated trade down on his desk, turns and leaves.

ANOTHER ANGLE
as Norma comes to take a spot beside her friend Bonnie Mae Buffum on the shuddering floor.

The inexorable work goes on, without end, without pause.

EXT. WITCHARD HOUSE
*Sonny drives up in his old Ford and gives one discreet BEEP on his horn.
Norma emerges on the front steps; holding each hand are Millie and Craig.
She marches them down to the car.*

> NORMA
> *(firmly)*

We're all ready.

> SONNY
> *(it's a bit more than he bargained for)*

All of you?

> NORMA

All three of us.

> SONNY
> *(with good grace)*

Well, then, everybody hop in.

MOVING SHOT—SONNY'S CAR

> NORMA

Roll the window down if you're hot.

> MILLIE

I wanna sit up front.

> NORMA

Well, you can't.

> CRAIG

Are we there yet?

> NORMA

No, we just started off.
> *(to Sonny)*
I thought we were going to the river.

> SONNY

We are. I gotta make a stop first.

EXT. BUNGALOW
*Sonny's car is at the curb in front of another house, Norma and her children
waiting impatiently.*

After a moment, Sonny emerges, a small girl's hand in his. He introduces her.

>   SONNY
> This is Alice. She's mine.

>   NORMA
>   *(laughs)*
> Like I always say—the more, the merrier.

Alice hops into the back with the boy and the girl. Off they go.

EXT. RIVERBANK
The kids play along the bank, clambering over a tree that spans the water. Norma and Sonny sit at a picnic table, hugging their knees, at ease with each other.

>   SONNY
> You're real easy with your kids.

>   NORMA
> Oh . . . I yell. I swat 'em.

>   SONNY
> You're a pretty woman.

>   NORMA
> I wasn't bad at eighteen. But things have slid and slipped . . .

>   SONNY
> You look fine to me.

>   NORMA
> Keep the lights low and I'm all right.

>   SONNY
> Well, I'll take you where it's dark.

>   NORMA
>   *(makes a weary wave with her hand)*
> I've been there.

Sonny is silent a moment.

>   SONNY
> I don't owe a nickel in this town. I'll eat anything that's put
> down in front of me. I can fix anything electrical. I'm all

right after I've had my first cup of coffee—I want that bad, though. I got me a new job at the gas station. I'd turn over my paycheck the minute I got it—that's Friday noon. And I come straight home from work and stay there.
> *(finally turns to look at her)*

I got me Alice and I'm alone. You got two kids and you're alone. If you could help me, maybe I could help you.

NORMA
It's been a long time between offers.
> *(she pauses)*

Well, kiss me. And, if that's all right, the rest'll be.

He takes her in his arms.

INT. LIVING ROOM
Belonging to the JUSTICE OF THE PEACE, stuffed with battered mohair furniture and family pictures. The wedding in progress is not overly festive: Norma holds a rather bedraggled little bouquet, but she is still a bird of plumage in her bright print dress. Once her mind is made up, she sweeps everything before her. The others, Sonny beside her, Bonnie Mae and Roscoe as witnesses, are slightly uncomfortable in unaccustomed finery.

JUSTICE OF THE PEACE
. . . And now, by the authority vested in me by this sovereign state, I pronounce you man and wife. If you like, you may kiss the bride.

Sonny kisses Norma tentatively.

JUSTICE OF THE PEACE
Mother over there has a glass of homemade wine for us. Picked the berries myself last summer.

They all turn to the little table on which his wife has prepared several tumblers and a bottle of red wine. Sonny raises his glass in a toast.

SONNY
To my wife, Norma Rae. I just hope I can keep up with her.

INT. WEAVING ROOM
Norma and Bonnie work side by side in the hellish din. Bonnie passes her a flyer. Norma unfolds it and reads:

TWUA MEETING TONIGHT AT THE CHOCKOYOTTE BAPTIST CHURCH.
IN YOUR INTEREST, COME HEAR REUBEN WARSHOVSKY, SPEAKER.

BONNIE
Roscoe says I shouldn't go, but I think I'm gonna.

NORMA
I'm not asking anybody. I'm going.

EXT. CHOCKOYOTTE CHURCH
as Norma and Bonnie walk up the rickety wooden steps and enter.

INT. THE CHURCH
*There are plain wooden walls, plain wooden pews, and a totally black
assembly. As the only white people, they are at first a little tentative, as if they
were intruding, and they halt in the entrance. A large, impressive man,
JAMES BROWN, waves them on in with his straw hat. They walk all the
way down to the front and sit in front of the altar, with its cross, a brightly
colored picture of Jesus, a jelly glass filled with wild flowers. The people wait
in silence, patiently.*

REUBEN
*He stands in front of the quiet, hopeful, needful people who have risked
something to be here. He speaks very simply.*

REUBEN
On October 4, 1970, my grandfather, Isaac Abraham
Warshovsky, aged 87, died in his sleep in New York City.
On the following Friday morning, his funeral was held. My
mother and father attended, my two uncles from Brooklyn
attended, my Aunt Minnie came up from Florida. Also
present were 862 members of The Amalgamated Clothing
Workers and The Cloth, Hat, and Cap Makers' Union.
Also members of his family. In death as in life, they stood
at his side. They had fought battles with him, bound the
wounds of battle with him, had earned bread together and
had broken it together. When they spoke, they spoke in one
voice, and they were heard. They were black, they were
white, they were Irish, they were Polish, they were Catholic,
they were Jews, they were one. That's what a union is: one.
(pauses)
Ladies and gentlemen, the textile industry, in which you are
spending your lives and your substance, and in which your

children and their children will spend their lives and substance, is the only industry in the whole length and breadth of the United States of America that is not unionized. Therefore, they are free to exploit you, to cheat you, to lie to you, and to take away what is rightfully yours—your health, a decent wage, a fit place to work. I would urge you to stop them by coming down to Room 31 at the Golden Cherry Motel to pick up a union card and sign it.
(pauses again)
It comes from the Bible—according to the tribes of your fathers, ye shall inherit. It comes from Reuben Warshovsky—not unless you make it happen.

He stops talking. The people have listened.

IN FRONT OF THE CHURCH
People are coming up to Reuben to shake his hand, to murmur words of appreciation. Bonnie Mae approaches.

BONNIE
Roscoe should've come. He should've heard you.

REUBEN
Bring him next time.

BONNIE
(agreeing)
If I have to drag him.

It is Norma's turn next. She stands in front of him with a slight grin.

NORMA
You preach pretty good.

REUBEN
When are you going to join up?

NORMA
Me? Who's got the time? I got my hands full as is.

REUBEN
(flat)
Make the time. Sleep less. If I don't get some help, it's kaput, finished, I'm out of town—and you got nothing.

ANOTHER ANGLE
He turns away from her and shakes hands with James Brown.

REUBEN
I'd appreciate any help you can give me. That's licking stamps, stuffing envelopes, typing with two fingers—anything.

JAMES
I'll show up.

Norma stands to the side, a little baffled, frustrated, uncertain.

THREE BOSSMEN
Three very grim, hard-faced men stand at the gate as the morning shift passes them: RICK LUJAN, DAN PETERS, WOODROW BOWZER. The mood is one of confrontation, testy, edgy, muscular.

ANOTHER ANGLE
They don't have long to wait. Reuben appears, dressed in tennis shoes, jeans and a golf cap, a large TWUA button on his chest. He is gulping his breakfast en route, a doughnut and a paper cup of coffee.

He steps up to the three men with a manner that is cool, firm, and peremptory.

REUBEN
Okay, I'm here, and I'm ready to look at your plant.

The three men just stand immobile, presenting a formidable barrier.

REUBEN
The federal government of the United States, brothers, in Federal Court Order Number 7778, states the following: the union has the right to inspect every bulletin board in the mills at least once a week, to verify in person that its notices are not being stripped off.

He is finished with the coffee and looks around.

REUBEN
You got a trash can?

Bowzer indicates one nearby with his granite jaw. Reuben tosses the empty cup into it.

REUBEN
Keep America beautiful.

They flank him and escort him inside.

IN THE MILL
The DIN is at full pitch, as always. LEROY MASON is waiting for them. He dispenses with greetings and hands Reuben a pair of earmuffs.

> REUBEN
> Thank you.

It is necessary for voices to be raised in order to be heard above the NOISE. They march, prison-style, Mason in front, Reuben in the center, the three bossmen bringing up the rear.

MOVING SHOT
Mason goes at quick-step, taking off at full speed. Reuben lets him go. After fifty feet, Mason stops, turns, sees that Reuben is not with him, and storms back.

> MASON
> Am I moving too quick for you or something?

> REUBEN
> I did my running when I was in the army. I'm not in the army now, brother.

> MASON
> Well, if you're out of shape, I'll slow down a little bit.

> REUBEN
> I'd appreciate it. Let's keep to a basic saunter.

ANOTHER ANGLE
The line of march begins again and Reuben swerves right out of it. He approaches JED BUFFUM at a loom.

> REUBEN
> Good morning. I'm Reuben Warshovsky of the Textile Workers' Union of America. What's your name, brother?

> BUFFUM
> *(uneasily)*
> Buffum.

> REUBEN
> How long you worked here, Mr. Buffum?

> BUFFUM

Twelve years.

> REUBEN

Like your job?

> BUFFUM

Like to keep it.

ANOTHER ANGLE
The cohort of bossmen surrounds him again.

> BOWZER

Warshovsky, you're interfering with the work, and the court order says you can't do that.

> REUBEN

Well, then, brother, let's both keep to the letter of the law.

> BOWZER
> *(mildly)*

I don't have no kike brother.

> REUBEN

I don't think you meant to use that word.

> BOWZER

Yeah, I did.

> REUBEN

Shit, now I gotta stop and get into a fight.

Mason steps between them.

> MASON

The bulletin board is right over there.

The words separate the two antagonists. Reuben turns and strides directly to it.

AT THE BULLETIN BOARD
He stands with his hands in his back pockets, rocking back and forth on his heels, looking at the board. The others come up behind him.

> REUBEN

Somebody's looking to get into a carpool . . . somebody wants to sell a bassett pup . . . and you can pick pecans at forty cents a bushel at Selma Landing . . .

(pauses)
Only thing missing is my notice.

LUJAN
It's there.

REUBEN
I don't see it.

The man points up high, to the very top of the board. Reuben's eyes follow his gesture.

REUBEN
Wilt Chamberlain on stilts could read it, maybe.
(voice hardens)
Put it at eye level, brothers, where everyone can read it.

MASON
We'll take note of your request.

REUBEN
(spreads his hands)
Why do you guys try this horseshit? Now I got to go to the phone and call my lawyers and get 'em on your ass. It's childish.
(turns to them)
Where's the pay phone and who's got two nickels?

MASON
(to Lujan, quietly)
Bring it down.

ANOTHER ANGLE
as Lujan scrapes a chair over, heaves his bulk up on it, pries out the thumbtacks while the other men stand watching, and puts it in a lower and more prominent position.

Reuben steps forward to read the notice carefully.

ANOTHER ANGLE
SAM BOLEN hurries over, wheezing hard and full of self-importance.

BOLEN

You're not supposed to read the damn thing!

REUBEN

No union organizer, not even a known union member, has been inside the fences or walls of this factory in more than ten years. I'm reading it.

BOLEN

Read fast.

REUBEN

While I'm reading this, tell you what—you go read the court order that says any agent of this company can be held in contempt. You're messing with a contempt citation, and if you're hot for jail, just keep it up.

BOLEN
(backing off)

I don't violate no laws.

REUBEN

Baby, you're violating the law now.

MASON

Can we finish this?

REUBEN

Where's the other board?

MASON

In the weaving room.

REUBEN

Show me.

MOVING SHOT

The contingent turns and marches across the length of the weaving room, over the bucking floor, through the snowstorm of lint, past workers who are alerted to his presence there, who turn over their shoulders to watch him, who exchange a furtive word. Reuben takes it all in; more than that, he draws attention to himself.

REUBEN

Hello, there . . . How are you this morning? . . . Warshovsky of the TWUA . . . 'Morning, ma'am, Reuben Warshovsky,

TWUA . . . Hello there, sir. I'm a union organizer, Golden
Cherry Motel downtown, door's always open . . .

NORMA
*Among those he passes is Norma. They exchange an especially significant
look.*

THE MARCH
*The company phalanx grows larger as they go, with each addition taller and
broader than Reuben.*

SECOND BULLETIN BOARD
*There are boxes and bolts of cloth arranged and stacked in such a way as to
block the board completely.*

*Confronted with the contempt the company has for its work force, the
obvious manipulation he sees, he stands thoughtfully a moment. It is beyond
anger or outburst.*

                          REUBEN
You know, gentlemen, your average working man isn't
stupid—he just gets tired.
                         (pauses)
Move that shit out of there.

*No one speaks. The bossmen form a semicircle behind Reuben. He is backed
up to the bulletin board.*

ANOTHER ANGLE
*James Brown and TWO OTHER BLACK MILL HANDS walk out between
the row of boxes. They stop and look. Mason looks at the black men, then at
his assistants.*

                          MASON
Move the stuff.

The bossmen wrestle the boxes and bolts away, clearing the board.

NORMA
watching. Interested, engrossed, making up her mind.

REUBEN'S MOTEL ROOM
*It is a shambles of abandoned meals, cartons, filing cabinets, empty Coke
bottles, dirty towels, shucked clothes, union applications, battered typewriter,
and just-washed T-shirts hanging, dripping on the floor, from chairs and
light fixtures.*

Reuben is wringing out a T-shirt when Norma approaches.

> NORMA
> *(knocking on the open door)*
> Hey, Reuben, you busy?

> REUBEN
> *(sarcastically, indicating the T-shirt)*
> Oh, yeah, very busy.

> NORMA
> Can I come in?

> REUBEN
> Please.

IN THE ROOM
She makes a slow turn, taking in the disorder.

> NORMA
> Don't they ever clean up in here?

> REUBEN
> *(impatiently)*
> I don't want 'em messing with my papers. I know where
> everything is.

She gives him a long, level look.

> NORMA
> If I joined up with you, would I lose my job?

> REUBEN
> No way! You can wear a union button as big as a frisbee
> when you go to work. You can talk union to any mill hand
> who wants to listen, as long as it's during a break. You can
> take union pamphlets to the mill and pass 'em along—and
> there's not a goddamn thing they can do to touch you.

> NORMA
> Well . . . I was never even in the Girl Scouts—but I'll go
> along with you.

> REUBEN
> *(pleased)*
> You're the fish I wanted to hook.

NORMA
(pauses)
Well . . . now you got me, what're you gonna do with me?

He is busy at the desk, scrabbling for application papers.

REUBEN
Make a mensch out of you.

NORMA
You are? What's that?

REUBEN
Somebody who goes to the Old Folks' Home on Saturday morning to visit instead of playing golf. Somebody who puts a dollar in a blind man's cup for a pencil.

NORMA
(confident of her worth)
I'd do that.

REUBEN
But would you take the pencil?

NORMA
'Course I would. I paid for it.

REUBEN
Between logic and charity falls a shadow. We could debate it all night.
(hands her a card)
Sign.

She signs her name with a flourish. He picks up the card and studies it.

REUBEN
Norma Rae Webster. How come everybody down here has three names?

LUNCHROOM
Norma, wearing a huge TWUA button, attempts to enlist WAYNE BILL-INGS over their coffee break. Booze and extra poundage are fast blurring his boyish good looks.

NORMA
(holding a button out)

Come on, Wayne, lemme pin it on you. It'll cover that gravy spot on your shirt.

WAYNE

What do I get if I do?

NORMA

You get *nothing* if you don't. Besides, haven't you had enough of that?

WAYNE

You and me used to heat up that N.C.O. Club down at the base. Remember?

NORMA

Bygone days.

WAYNE

Well, pin it on me for bygone days, then.

NORMA

Stand still.

She pins the large button on him.

WAYNE

Think we'll ever see that club again, Norma, honey?

NORMA

Take your wife—she doesn't get out much.

She walks out quickly.

ON THE FLOOR
Lujan, the bossman, bars her way.

LUJAN

Looks like you strayed off the reservation, Norma.

NORMA

Is that right?

LUJAN

You got your own coffee machine at your end.

NORMA
Yeah, but I ain't got a water fountain at my end, and I gotta
cool my coffee down before I drink it.

LUJAN
(flatly)
You cool *everything* down.

She swings her hips as she walks away from him.

EXT. CHURCH
*The white church is a bit larger, in somewhat better repair than Chockoyotte.
The REVEREND WAYNE HUBBARD, though minister to this flock, does
its menial as well as its spiritual work and with brush in hand is busy painting
the iron stair rail as Norma approaches.*

HUBBARD
You caught me in my shirtsleeves, Norma.

NORMA
Reverend.

HUBBARD
Maybe we could have some flowers out of your yard for
Sunday, Norma. I got spider mite eating up everything.

NORMA
Okay.

HUBBARD
(after a pause)
Can I help you with something?

NORMA
How long have I been coming to this church, Reverend?

HUBBARD
Since you were a little girl.

NORMA
That's right. I accepted Christ when I was six years old.
Would you call me a good Christian?

HUBBARD
With a lapse or two, I'd say so.

NORMA
Would you call yourself a good Christian?

HUBBARD
That's for the Lord to say.

NORMA
I want this church for a union meeting next Saturday afternoon. That's blacks and whites, sitting together.

He stops his work.

HUBBARD
This is a house of God.

NORMA
That's what I'm waiting to see—if it is or it isn't.

HUBBARD
You're coming close to blasphemy, Norma.

NORMA
I've come here and I've said that I've sinned and I've done wrong and I'm sorry and I want God to forgive me. Now I want to see what this church stands for. I want to see if you'll stand up in that pulpit and say there should be justice, there should be a union, if you're oppressed, fight back, if you're smitten, rise up—and the Lord'll be on your side. If you don't do that, I say there's nothing in this church that's any good to me and I'll leave it flat.

HUBBARD
We'll miss your voice in the choir, Norma.

NORMA
You'll hear it raised up someplace else.

And she turns on her heel and walks away.

SONNY'S HOUSE
Norma pulls into the driveway behind Reuben's car, parks and gets out, four black men and one white emerging with her. She says to them:

NORMA
You all go in and sit down. I'll be right there.

Then she turns purposefully and walks directly across the street.

NORMA AND DAN PETERS
Peters sits on his front porch, smoking a cigarette, studying the activity in front of him.

Norma comes up to the man.

> NORMA
> We're holding a meeting at my house, Dan. Union business and then lemonade and cookies. Gingersnaps. I'll roll up the front shade so you can see right in. Washed my windows Saturday so you shouldn't have any trouble.

Norma sails back across the driveway to her house.

AT HER DOOR
Sonny is waiting for her, perturbed.

> SONNY
> You're going too far now, Norma. This here is where we live.

> NORMA
> How'm I going too far?

> SONNY
> Bunch of black men in there . . . you're gonna get us in a lot of trouble.

> NORMA
> I never had any trouble with the black men. Only trouble I ever had in my life was with white men.

She goes inside.

INT. LIVING ROOM
Reuben is already present, together with another handful of mill hands, black and white. Among those who have come are James Brown, Lucius White, Bonnie Mae and Roscoe, Mavis Pruitt.

They are seated on the sofa and on wooden chairs lined around in a circle. A few men stand against the wall, holding their caps in their hands.

There is no sense of being ill at ease; only of gravity, fatigue, need. Reuben speaks:

REUBEN

I remember some of you from the Chockoyotte Church . . .
I did all the talking that day. I'd like you to talk now.

*There is silence a moment. ABNER SACKS looks around the circle, clears
his throat.*

SACKS

A man's work should be a man's work—not a term in jail.

*VELMA STACKHOUSE, work-worn, smooths the folds in her lap, reluctant
to speak. But she does so.*

VELMA STACKHOUSE

Excuse me for saying this with men folks in the room, but
when I get my menstrual cramps, which come pretty hard,
they don't let me sit down on the job.

LOUISE PICKENS

They say you gotta keep to your feet unless you bring a
note from the doctor. We wouldn't say we was sick if we
wasn't.

JAMES BROWN

I look at a brick wall all day. Used to be a window there,
but they come and bricked it up to give us the feeling we're
shut in.

LINETTE ODUM

My husband Averill died of brown lung two months ago.
His children're going to grow up without knowing him. I got
all his clothes if someone could use 'em.

INT. KITCHEN
*Later. Norma and Reuben are alone. She has brewed a pot of coffee. He is
hunched over his cup, dissatisfied.*

REUBEN

I'm not getting the message across. Seventeen people out of
eight hundred.

NORMA

You're an outsider. Down here things take time. This isn't
New York, where you grab a taxi and grab your hat . . .

ANOTHER ANGLE
They are interrupted by the appearance of a very sleepy Millie in the doorway.

                    MILLIE
    Momma, Craig is wetting the bed.

                    NORMA
                (as she goes)
    I told him not to drink Coke before he went to sleep.
                (to the boy)
    Craig, come on sugar, wake up. Put your arms around my
    neck. That-a boy.

Reuben sits a moment, then rises to follow her.

HALLWAY
*He wanders after her, still sipping from his cup. He continues talking to her
through the open door to the bathroom, where she kneels and supports a still
sleeping Craig on the toilet. A little TINKLING SOUND accompanies their
talk.*

                    REUBEN
    We've got to get this thing moving. It's bogging down on
    me.

                    NORMA
    Buy a jug of corn whiskey and pick me up on Saturday.
    We'll hit the back roads.
                (looks down)
    Finished, honey?

*Craig nods once and his head falls to his chest. She hoists him off the toilet,
pulls up his pajamas, lifts him in her arms.*

MONTAGE
A. BESIDE A TRACTOR
*old and mud-splattered. DUDLEY ROBINSON is changing a tire when
Norma and Reuben approach.*

                    NORMA
    Howdy, Mr. Robinson. How are you doing today?

                    ROBINSON
    I'm busy.

                          NORMA
I'm Norma Rae. You know me.

                          ROBINSON
                          (standing now to face them)
How do you do?

                          NORMA
This is my friend Reuben.

                          REUBEN
                          (handing him a flier)
Listen, sir, why don't you read this, and I'll change your
tire? How about that?

                          ROBINSON
You've got a deal.

Norma and Reuben crouch down next to the tractor's wheel.

                          REUBEN
You know how to do this?

                          NORMA
Are you kiddin'? I don't even got a car.

                          REUBEN
Well, let's look like we know what we're doing.

Reuben turns the monkey wrench in one direction . . .

                          NORMA
Reuben, I think he was taking this thing off.

. . . and then the other.

B. A COUNTRY STORE
*on the outskirts of town. Saturday leisure for half a dozen men from the mill
consists of sitting or squatting on the gallery of the store with pocketknives
and chunks of wood. Reuben puts his foot up on the porch while Norma
takes an RC Cola out of the ice chest and cools down.*

*In a gesture calculated to make him one of them, Reuben takes out a
penknife, pries open a blade, and begins to whittle as he addresses the men.
Chips fly off his stick as he becomes animated. The men listen impassively. Before he knows it, Reuben has whittled his stick down to a toothpick—
and he cuts his finger.*

WHITTLER
I'm damn glad you did that.

C. A YARD
A mill worker keeps chickens in a roost and a single dairy cow. As Reuben nears, he trips and falls into a pile of dung—and is splattered from chin to boots. Norma offers a laconic comment.

NORMA
It's only grass and water, Reuben . . .

AT A SWIMMING HOLE
a little river running through sand and clay, the grass spotted with blue and white daisies, sheltered by a row of sedge. The sun is high, the air still, and Reuben is in the water, rolling and snorting, naked, content.

ANOTHER ANGLE
Norma is downstream a little on the bank, vigorously scrubbing his soiled clothes. She looks up at him.

NORMA
This is where we used to swim when we were kids. We'd hookey off from school, come down here, shuck our clothes and jump in.

REUBEN
The only water I ever saw when I was a kid was when we opened a fire hydrant on 110th Street with a monkey wrench.

He floats on his back, very much at peace with the world.

REUBEN
Ahh . . . this is the life.

NORMA
It's just a mudhole.

REUBEN
It's cooling off my mosquito bites.

NORMA
She wrings out the wet jeans and then spreads them on a rock.

NORMA
That's as clean as they're gonna get.

Then she leans back on her heels, wipes the sweat from her face.

NORMA

God, it's hot . . . I'm coming in.

She gets up and begins to shed her clothes matter-of-factly.

REUBEN

He swims about lazily, enjoying himself. When he turns again, Norma is in the water near him.

REUBEN AND NORMA

They tread water in place, hardly rippling the surface, quiet, cooling down.

NORMA

There used to be a farmer around here with a B-B gun. I hope he's moved.

REUBEN

There's something flicking around my toes.

NORMA

Minnows. They won't hurt you.
(grins a little)
You're sure a fish out of water down here, aren't you?

REUBEN

It's not exactly my native habitat.

NORMA

What would you do at home on a day like this?

REUBEN

Play some handball at the Y. Go see Aida at the Met. Eat Chinese. Get in a poker game. Hit the sack.

NORMA

I've been two places in my life. Millageville and Piston.

REUBEN

You'd love New York. It's a super town. Most beautiful women in the world . . . best food . . . opera . . . theater . . . ballet . . .

NORMA

Reuben, you're homesick.

REUBEN

Oh, boy.

NORMA

Reuben, you got a skinny build.

REUBEN

Yeah.

NORMA

Sonny works out with weights.

REUBEN

I tried that. Dropped them and broke my foot.

NORMA

Well, you don't have to worry. You got a head on you, and you use it.

And with this, they swim apart.

INT. KITCHEN

Norma is on the phone, a long checklist of names on a pad in front of her, most of them already crossed off. She is wearing a nightgown; there is a pencil in her disordered hair.

NORMA

. . . Sure, I know why we got a bad connection—they probably got a tap on my phone. Hey, you! You listening? This is Norma Rae Webster, talking union to Henry Willis.

Sonny, rumpled, aggrieved, wearing shorts, appears in the doorway and stands watching his wife.

NORMA

I'm on tonight and every night, no commercials, same old story, union, union, union. Tell your bossman to tape me and you can go on home to your wife and kids.

(then)

Henry, you still there?

The line BUZZES in her ear, the connection broken.

NORMA

Damn!

She hangs up angrily, sits fuming a moment, then yanks out the pencil, puts a question mark after Henry's name, finally becomes aware of her husband in the doorway.

ANOTHER ANGLE
as Sonny speaks shortly.

> SONNY
>
> You ain't getting any sleep and I ain't getting any sleep and we both gotta go to work in the morning.

> NORMA
>
> I got a hundred names to call here.

> SONNY
>
> That gonna go on our phone bill?

> NORMA
>
> It'll come out of *my* paycheck, how's that?

ANOTHER ANGLE
He doesn't answer, pads past her to the refrigerator, pours a glass of cold milk, takes a mouthful, makes a face, sloshes the rest into the sink.

> SONNY
>
> This milk's sour.

> NORMA
>
> I didn't get to the market.

> SONNY
> *(goading)*
>
> You didn't get to the market and you didn't get to the washing and you didn't get to the kids and you didn't get to me.

> NORMA
> *(with icy calm)*
>
> Is that right?

> SONNY
> *(raging on)*
>
> We're eating them frozen TV dinners, the kids are going around in dirty jeans, and I'm going *without* altogether!

ANOTHER ANGLE
Norma pushes back from the table, making a very large show of it.

NORMA
Okay. You want cooking? You *got* cooking.

There is a tremendous clatter as she yanks open cupboard doors and pots tumble out in every direction, strewn by the fury of her gesture. She slams one on the stove, grabs a hunk of meat and some cabbage from the refrigerator, throws the meat into the pot, adds water, whacks the cabbage in half, tosses that in as well, bangs the lid on top of it.

She whirls on Sonny again.

NORMA
You want laundry? You *got* laundry.

ANOTHER ANGLE
She opens a bin stuffed to the brim with dirty clothes. She hauls out a huge armload, dumps it in the sink, runs the tap water, pours liquid soap over it. She faces Sonny once more.

NORMA
You want ironing? You *got* ironing!

She snatches up a shirt out of a basket of unironed clothes, pulls open a cupboard door, wrestles out the ironing board, kicks it vehemently into an upright position, grabs an iron, jams it into a plug. She spreads out the shirt, spits on her finger and tests the iron's heat, begins making furious swipes. Over her shoulder she hurls a final question at Sonny:

NORMA
You wanna make love? Get behind me and lift my skirt and we'll make love!

ANOTHER ANGLE
as Sonny stands looking at her, half-admiring, certainly defeated.

SONNY
Norma, Norma . . .

EXT. MILL
During break time, Norma passes among the mill hands with a sheaf of leaflets, handing them out. She comes suddenly face-to-face with her father.

VERNON
Well, I don't bump into you much these days.

> NORMA

Are you all right, Daddy?

> VERNON

About the same.

> NORMA

You color's bad. Have you been drinking?

> VERNON

Oh, I take a thimbleful or so.

> NORMA

It's not good for you.

> VERNON

What's the difference, honey? I'm beginning to wonder when I lie down if I'm gonna get up.

> NORMA

Don't talk old to me. I don't like it.

She embraces him fiercely, touched by a strange foreboding.

> VERNON

One of these nights I'm gonna come by and take you to a grand dinner . . .

> NORMA

I'd like that.

INT. MOTEL ROOM

It is late. Reuben sits with his legs on the desk, studying briefs; Norma is at a typewriter at another desk, pecking away with two fingers. She pauses to erase away, pecks again, makes another mistake, erases, pulls the paper out, crumples it up and throws it down. She yawns widely.

> REUBEN
> *(without looking up)*

James.

> NORMA

He went home an hour ago.

He grunts, goes back to his reading.

> NORMA

I oughta be going home.

She gets up, rubs her back, goes to the open window, gets a deep breath of air.

ANOTHER ANGLE
As she turns back, she notes that a new picture of Dorothy Finkelstein has arrived. She goes to it idly.

NORMA
How's Dorothy?

REUBEN
(absorbed in his reading)
Fine.

NORMA
I see you got another picture.

REUBEN
My mother sent it.

NORMA
I bet she gets along with your mother.

He finally looks up.

REUBEN
Are you kidding? My mother loves her. She's a lawyer, she's Jewish, she's a lefto, and she's a great cook. What the hell else could she want?

She puts the picture down, stares at it a moment longer. She seems a little wistful.

NORMA
How'd she get to be so smart?

REUBEN
Books.

He rummages in one of a half dozen brown paper bags, looking for food, comes up with two bananas. He peels one and offers it to her.

Another bag yields a final can of beer. He pulls the tab, holds it out while it foams, drinks deeply.

ANOTHER ANGLE
She wanders past the row of books he has strewn about, picks one up at random.

                    NORMA
Who's Dylan Thomas?

                    REUBEN
A poet, a drunk, a genius.

                    NORMA
What does he write about?

                    REUBEN
Love, sex, death, and other matters of consequence.

                    NORMA
Is he hard to read?

                    REUBEN
Yeah.

                    NORMA
Then why should I bother?

                    REUBEN
'Cause he's got something to say.
                    (quotes)
"Rage, rage against the dying of the light."

                    NORMA
I'll try him. Hell, there's nothing but reruns on television.

                    REUBEN
Do me a favor. Don't eat while you read. I can't stand
banana in my books.

                    NORMA
                    (as she leaves)
Kvetch, kvetch, kvetch!

EXT. CHURCH
Reuben opens the door to the Chockoyotte Church and enters.

INT. CHURCH
*It is empty. A kitten has gotten in and picks its way along the altar, pausing
to lift its head and stare at the intruder.*

*Baffled, Reuben sits down in a pew at the back and waits. A cause, a man,
and a cat.*

LATTING HOUSE
Reuben pulls up in front of a ramshackle home, its paint worn down to gray board, a step or two broken, the porch listing, an abandoned mattress falling apart in the yard. He knocks.

ANOTHER ANGLE
as Warren Latting opens the door. The man is still work-stained from his day at the mill, hollow-eyed, exhausted.

REUBEN
Nobody showed at the meeting today. What's going on?

WARREN
They got us on a stretch-out. Put us on a three-day week. Twice as much work and half the pay. On account of you. You just stand there a minute.

ANOTHER ANGLE
He disappears, leaving Reuben to cool his heels on the porch. In a moment he is back with a steaming pot in his hand. He lifts the lid.

WARREN
There's six turnips and two quarts of water in there. Supper for seven people. Go sell your union someplace else.

He kicks the door shut in Reuben's face.

INT. BOBBIN ROOM
Vernon works at an accelerated clip, transferring bobbins from one bin to another. He is like a man at stoop labor, bending, rising, bending, rising.

ANOTHER ANGLE
as Vernon's arm suddenly goes stiff. He kneels down.

Jimmy Jerome Davis comes over, puts his face close so he can hear.

VERNON
My arm's gone numb on me, Jimmy. I think I'd better go and lie down.

JIMMY
You got a break coming up in fifteen minutes, Vernon.

VERNON
I think I'd better go now.

JIMMY
You hold on, Vernon. Your break's coming up.

He pats Vernon on the back and walks on.

VERNON
He tries to resume his work but falls into the bin of bobbins. They swallow up his inert body.

GRAVEYARD
Like everything else in Henleyville, the graveyard is hard, harsh, graves wrested out of rocky soil. People who have spent their lives in unremitting work come to a stony resting place here.

Norma, Leona, the children, Sonny, uncomfortable in dark clothes, sit by the open grave as the pine box is lowered.

INT. BATHROOM OF REUBEN'S MOTEL
Every inch of space is now in full use; even the bathtub is crammed with cartons and papers.

PULL BACK
Somehow a card table has been wedged into the bathroom and two girls sit facing each other at typewriters, hard at it.

INT. MOTEL ROOM
A dozen people fill the single motel room, stuffing envelopes, addressing them, checking off lists, on the telephones.

PETER GALLAT comes through the door, and Norma, looking up from her work table, attacks him immediately.

NORMA
You get off your shift at three, you're supposed to be here at three-fifteen, and it's four-fifteen! Where the hell you been? You working for this union or aren't you?

PETER
I was getting my tooth filled.

NORMA
You were getting your beer gut filled!

PETER
Chew your old man out at home and get off me, Norma.

> NORMA

I'm just starting on you. I'm giving nine, ten, eleven, twelve hours. And that's every day! There's a pile of work around here. We're doing our piece of it, you do your piece of it—or don't call yourself a union member!

ANOTHER ANGLE

Reuben unwinds himself from his crowded desk, rises slowly and walks over. Norma finds herself face-to-face with him.

> REUBEN
> *(coldly)*

Shut your cake-hole, Norma.

Her face mirrors her astonishment at his sudden, brusque attack.

> REUBEN

In fact, get the hell out of the office.

> NORMA

What did *I* do? I just said what was *so*.

From its cacophony of SOUND, the room has suddenly BECOME VERY STILL. Reuben shows her his thumb, jabbing it toward the door.

> REUBEN

Out.

For a moment, she does nothing. Then, quite simply, she turns to look for her purse, picks it up and walks out. The silence in the room persists.

INT. COFFEE SHOP

In the shop attached to the motel, Norma sits alone over a cup of coffee and a wedge of pie. But the food remains untouched before her. She is thinking.

The door swings open, and Reuben enters, looking around. He sees her and ambles over.

> REUBEN
> *(as he sits at the counter next to her)*

Mouth.

She says nothing.

> REUBEN

You're too muscular. You can't come down that hard on a man and leave him his balls. Easy, Norma. Jesus. If you were in the State Department, we'd be at war.

He takes her fork, samples her pie, likes it, pulls it toward him and begins to eat.

> NORMA
> You're right. I got a big mouth.
> *(pauses)*
> You know, cotton mill workers are known as trash to some, and I know this union is the only way we can get our voice and make ourselves better. I guess that's why I push.

> REUBEN
> Our own Mother Jones.

> NORMA
> Who's she?

> REUBEN
> She was a considerable lady. She made it happen for coal miners in West Virginia.

> NORMA
> Then you're not sore at me?

> REUBEN
> If the situation called for a smart, loud, profane, sloppy, hard-working woman, I'd pick you every time out.

> NORMA
> *(after a moment)*
> How come sloppy? Nobody wears a girdle anymore.

But she is pleased and placated.

ANOTHER ANGLE
The waitress is at the counter, holding a check.

> REUBEN
> *(rising)*
> Give it to her. I didn't order anything.

> NORMA
> Well, hell, you ate it.

But he is already striding out the door, going back to work. Norma rummages in her purse for some change.

INT. REUBEN'S OFFICE
It is late and Norma, exhausted, has thrown clutter off the bed, curled up on it and fallen into a deep sleep.

ANOTHER ANGLE
She awakens with a start to find two strangers standing in the doorway and looking down at her. Norma stands.

> NORMA
> Who are you looking for?

The two men are present on business and have no time for amenities.

> LONDON
> Warshovsky around?

> NORMA
> He's at the printer's.

> LONDON
> Pretty late for the printer's . . .

> NORMA
> Reuben keeps him working late.

> DAKIN
> You're Norma Rae, aren't you?

> NORMA
> *(sensing hostility)*
> I'm Missus Webster.

> DAKIN
> We're from the union. National headquarters.
> *(points to the other man)*
> Al London. And I'm Sam Dakin.

> NORMA
> As long as you're here, I'll give you my shopping list. We need envelopes, we need typing paper, we need stamps, we need a loudspeaker, we could use a couple more typewriters that don't stick.

> LONDON
> We're not in office supplies, Missus Webster.

NORMA

You're not around much, either.

ANOTHER ANGLE
as Reuben walks in. If he is surprised to see the men, he doesn't show it.
They shake hands all around.

REUBEN

How are you, Sam? You've gotten fat.

DAKIN

Yeah, I put on a couple of pounds.

REUBEN

How are you, Al?

LONDON

Lousy, I got a cold.

There is an awkward pause.

REUBEN

What brings you?

LONDON

You're not getting up much of a head of steam, Reuben.

REUBEN

You've had my reports. You know what I'm up against.

DAKIN

We're worried.

REUBEN

That makes three of us.

DAKIN

This is a small Baptist Southern town. We have to keep our
noses very clean.

REUBEN
(reacting to the pressure)

You see any snot on mine?

DAKIN

Maybe Missus Webster would like to leave?

ANOTHER ANGLE
as Norma turns to go. Reuben raises a hand. She stops in her tracks.

REUBEN
Why should she leave?

DAKIN
This concerns her. I'm trying to make it easy for her.

REUBEN
(irritably)
Come on, come on, it's late. What is it?

DAKIN
The company wants us to look bad. They're going to use everything they can to make us look bad. You know, these mill hands go to church every Sunday, and she's talking union to 'em.
(pauses slightly)
They say she was in a porno movie, with a member of the local police department. Very explicit.

REUBEN
Show it to me. Run it for me.

DAKIN
There doesn't have to be a movie if there's talk that there is one. This lady has had an illegitimate child. She's slept around. She takes naps on your bed late at night.

REUBEN
I don't deserve this. Are we in the character assassination business or are we in the union business? All of a sudden, after I've put in an eighteen-hour day, I got the legion of decency on my hands! She's been breaking her ass for this organization. She doesn't see her kids, she doesn't have time to take a bath! What the fuck do I care if she's got round heels? Is this the Catholic Church? . . . Are we going to canonize her?

DAKIN
This is your show, Reuben . . . but maybe she ought to go.

REUBEN
Make it stick. If you can't, get out of here.

(throws open the door)
Get out of here anyway.

DAKIN
(to Norma)
I'm sorry about this, Missus Webster.

He motions to London. The two men leave.

ANOTHER ANGLE
Norma and Reuben are alone in the room. She is grateful for his defense but aware of the gravity of the situation. Neither speaks a moment.

NORMA
I wouldn't hurt the union. If you want me to quit, I will.

REUBEN
(irritably)
How come you were sleeping? I asked you to type those letters.

She goes to the typewriter, rubbing a sore spot in her back.

CLOSE SHOT
Jimmy Jerome Davis is tacking up a notice on the bulletin board in the weaving room. Very large black letters command the reader: "ALL EMPLOYEES ATTENTION."

PHONE BOOTH
An agitated Norma is on the phone, impatiently listening to the RINGS. At last the other end is picked up.

NORMA
It's me, Norma. All right, it is *I*, Norma. Forget the grammar—I gotta see you right away. Meet me on my break.

She hangs up, steps out, comes face-to-face with Tommy Gardner. She speaks to him airily.

NORMA
Calling my kids to see if they got home from school.

TOMMY
(nailing the lie)
Your kids are in the grocery store with my kids, buying candy. They do it every day.

NORMA
Maybe that's why my dentist's bills are busting me.

And she walks back to work.

A YARD
A fight breaks out, one of the white workers rounding on a black, sending him dazed to his knees with a violent blow. The black is up instantly and at the white: a close-in, savage fight. In the next moment, the confrontation expands; four whites join in, half a dozen blacks meet them, more whites advance. There is now a general melee in the yard. There is an uproar as each side champions its own.

Company men come on the run to quell it.

AT THE FENCE—MOVING SHOT
Norma and Reuben meet. They prowl the fence between them.

REUBEN
What started it?

NORMA
They put up a letter. They're telling the whites that the blacks are gonna run the union, take it over and push 'em around. You tell a white man that a black man is gonna sit on his head—
(gestures)
—and this is what you get.

REUBEN
I like it when those pricks get mean. We can take legal action. Get me the letter.

NORMA
I can't just waltz in and take it off the board. They're watching.

REUBEN
How good's your memory?

NORMA
Well—I still don't know the whole salute to the flag.

REUBEN
Get somebody to help you. Learn a line at a time. Write it down.

> NORMA
> *(hesitates a moment)*

It reminds me of the time I pinched a lipstick out of the five and dime.

> REUBEN

Did you get caught?

> NORMA

No. I went back the next week for curlers.

> REUBEN

Then you ought to know how.

They separate, each going quickly.

INT. SHEARING HALL

Sipping from a paper cup on her coffee break, Norma saunters toward the bulletin board and past it. She turns with elaborate nonchalance, comes back and stops in front of it. She reads quickly, then shuts her eyes tight, her mouth moving. She hits her head with the palm of her hand, as if to drive the information home. Then she hurries to the ladies' room.

INT. LADIES' ROOM

Norma is busy leaning on the sink, writing on a piece of toilet paper with an eyebrow pencil.

> NORMA
> *(muttering)*

". . . You black employees are being told that by going into the union in mass you can dominate it and control it in this plant as you may see fit. If now . . ."
> *(hesitates)*

". . . If now . . ."
> *(lost it)*

Damn! What's next? I can't remember.

CLOSE SHOT

A long strip of toilet paper with a black scrawl from one end to the other.

PULL BACK

It is night. Reuben is holding Norma's transcription at arm's length, reading it. He puts it down and turns to her.

> REUBEN

Where's the rest?

NORMA

That's the most I could get.

REUBEN

Mata Hari.

NORMA

They were watching us every minute.

He sees the futility of it and his voice hardens.

REUBEN

It's the best chance we've got to nail these bastards, to get 'em with their pants down. Don't tell me you can't remember it, you can't get it. Walk up to it, stand there, copy it down, word for word, line for line. Get the date, get the signature, get it all—and get it back to me!

NORMA

I'll get fired.

REUBEN

I'll run you a benefit.

She gives him an odd look. She has had a hard line from men before.

NORMA

Thanks a lot.

He is excited, goaded, tired, tense. Things are coming to a head.

REUBEN

If you want to get massaged, go to a massage parlor. You either get licked or you don't get licked.

NORMA

Listen. I got three kids. I got a drawer full of bills. I got a husband doesn't like what I'm doing. I'll do it. But I don't need your boot on my backside, Mister Warshovsky.

ANOTHER ANGLE

He pours himself a cup of coffee from the plug-in coffee maker, stands looking down into it.

REUBEN

Goddamn sludge has been standing here for three days . . .

There is a silence. She looks at him calmly, coolly.

NORMA

I'm going to tell you something, Reuben.

REUBEN

What are you going to tell me, Norma?

NORMA

You been away from home a long time. You been all business. You're getting crabby. You need a woman.

REUBEN

Funny you should mention it. Tonight's the night.

He puts down the cup, yanks his jacket off the back of a chair, struggles into it. He starts for the door.

She can't resist a parting shot.

NORMA

I wonder what Dorothy'd say.

REUBEN

Wear a rubber.

He slams out.

NORMA

Clipboard in hand, she goes straight to the bulletin board. She writes briskly, snatching a phrase off the letter with a glance, then looking down as her hand scrawls quickly. In order to transcribe accurately, she pronounces each phrase aloud.

NORMA
(quoting)

". . . that where unions are strikes occur. Strikes mean loss of work, loss of pay, and often loss of jobs . . . Strike and trouble, which often end up in serious violence . . ."

ANOTHER ANGLE
Rick Lujan is beside her. He means business.

LUJAN

You can't take down that letter.

NORMA

It's up here on the bulletin board—and I'm gonna copy it.

Dan Peters joins them.

PETERS
Norma, you better not.

NORMA
(dogged)
Dan, I'm gonna take down every word of this letter. It's my break time, and I'm gonna take down every word of this letter.

He reaches out as if to take her arm and stop her, but she pulls away fiercely.

NORMA
Just keep out of my way! I'm gonna take down this letter!

Now Leroy Mason approaches.

MASON
Hello, Norma.

NORMA
Why, Mr. Mason, you know who I am.

MASON
Norma, you just put your pencil and paper away.

She ignores him and continues to write as rapidly as she can.

MASON
You just stop what you're doing—right now—'cause you're about to leave.

She whirls around.

NORMA
You better not put a hand on me.

ANOTHER ANGLE
as the three men take a step back, two of them looking at Mason to see what to do next.

MASON
The law's coming and it's gonna take you right out of the plant.

NORMA
Mr. Mason, I started this and—I'm gonna finish this—

The three men are stunned into silence and inactivity. She turns back to the board and calmly finishes her task. Then she folds her notes, shoves them in her pocket.

ANOTHER ANGLE

> PETERS
> Let's go to the office, Norma.

She goes with the two men, back across the long hall, people turning to watch.

A number of men are arrayed in force against her: Lujan, Peters, Moody, Alston, Mason. Mason descends on her sternly.

> MASON
> Why did you make personal phone calls on company time?

By way of reply she suddenly whips out pencil and paper.

> NORMA
> I'd like you to spell out your name for me.

> MASON
> *(interrupting)*
> Now you're being foolish, Norma Rae.

She drops the pencil and paper in her lap, puts her hands over her ears and closes her eyes, embattled.

> NORMA
> Look, Mr. Mason, nobody's on my side around here, and I'm not gonna leave until I set down all your names on this piece of paper.

> MASON
> *(exploding)*
> I don't want you on the premises. You make a phone call to your husband and tell him to come fetch you. I want you out of here right quick.

She gets up without another word and walks out of the office.

She goes back to the looms but she does no work. She merely stands there. Everyone on the floor stands in silence, attentive. The room is charged with tension.

ANOTHER ANGLE
A PINKERTON MAN in uniform comes toward her. When he is about ten feet away, she raises her hand. He stops.

> NORMA
> *(singing it out)*
> Forget it. I'm staying put—right where I am.

The man shrugs, turns and leaves. She looks around the floor. All eyes are on her. She stands rigid.

ANOTHER ANGLE
There is a SOUND of a DOOR SLAMMING, a GREAT METALLIC CLANG. Now a CITY POLICEMAN is warily approaching her. She waits until he is close and then she shouts, so that the man is halted in his tracks.

> NORMA
> It's gonna take you and the police department and the fire department and the National Guard to get me out of here.

The policeman hesitates, vacillates, then takes another rather uncertain step or two forward. Norma, concerned, backs away.

> NORMA
> I'm waiting on the Sheriff to come drive me home, and I'm not budging until he arrives.

But the policeman continues to shuffle toward her.

ANOTHER ANGLE
At bay, surrounded, alone, the pressure intense, she suddenly reaches around behind her and fumbles for a sheet of stiff cardboard. She grabs lipstick, and with one eye on the policeman, she strikes off some heavy block letters on the cardboard. Then with one thrust, she hoists herself up on top of a table and stands on it.

REVERSE SHOT
Everyone on the floor is watching her, Bonnie close to tears, Leona shaken and tense, James Brown, George Hubbard, Ray Buck, frustrated, immobilized, awaiting the outcome.

NORMA
She holds her sign over her head with both hands and slowly turns in a circle so that everyone on the open floor, all focused entirely on her, can read what she has written:

UNION

THE MILL HANDS
It is as if her upraised sign is an igniting torch to the blaze that follows. Slowly, gradually, they turn off their machines. The first to do so is Norma's mother. The man next to her follows suit. James Brown shuts his down. Lucius White is next. Then George Hubbard.

One by one, they join in, until the room falls silent.

ANOTHER ANGLE
Norma looks down to see the bossmen, the Pinkerton, and LAMAR MILLER, chief of police. He calls up to her.

> MILLER
> Come on down here, Norma Rae. It's no good your standing there.

ANOTHER ANGLE
Norma doesn't answer. She continues to turn slowly, showing her sign.

NORMA
Finished, she climbs down.

> NORMA
> *(fixing him)*
> Lamar, before I budge from here, you're gonna put into writing that Sheriff Lamar Miller will take Norma Rae Webster straight home. You sign it and give me that piece of paper.

> MILLER
> Don't tell me what to do, young lady. You're not gonna get anything in writing off of me.
> *(turns to Mason)*
> You want her removed from the premises?

> MASON
> Get her out of here.

Miller turns back to Norma.

> MILLER
> I don't know that I want to get into that automobile with you and nobody else.

NORMA
Lamar, I'm not gonna bite you.

ANOTHER ANGLE
Norma turns and leads the way, Miller, the policeman, and the Pinkerton behind her.

EXT. MILL
As they emerge, Norma sees two cars in front of her, an unmarked car and a police car. She stops short.

NORMA
That's a police car! You're taking me to jail!

Behind her she hears the chain link fence beginning to close. She spins around, races for the fence, grips the gate fiercely.

The policeman and the Pinkerton are after her.

POLICEMAN
Now quit that scrapping. You're going where I take you— and that's to jail.

They grab her arms, pry her fingers loose, wrench her away. Holding her by the arms, they rush her to the police cruiser, shoving her head down, stuffing her into the back seat, slamming the door.

INT. CAR
She looks around, feeling trapped.

There are no door handles, no window cranks. A thick wire mesh separates her from the front seat.

Miller and the policeman get in the front, the latter breathing heavily from his exertion. The car pulls away, the dark bulk of the mill looming behind them.

INT. JAIL
Norma's face is impassive as she listens to Miller dictating the warrant for her arrest.

MILLER
Webster, Norma Rae. 704 Crester Road, Henleyville. Female. White. Thirty-one. Occupation: textile. Dark complexion. Brown hair. Brown eyes. Arrest number: 2238-B. Charge: disorderly conduct.

INT. JAIL
A heavyset MATRON appears. Miller turns away from the desk sergeant to Norma.

MILLER
You go with her, Norma.

Wordlessly, she follows the matron.

MOVING SHOT
as she is led past the drunk tank, past a row of empty cells to her own. It is ten feet long, five feet wide, a dim light burning in it, bunk beds, a toilet, a wash basin.

THE CELL
She steps inside.

MATRON
You might as well sit down.

Miller appears in the doorway.

MILLER
You got one phone call, Norma. You better call Sonny.

NORMA
I'm calling my union organizer.

MILLER
Here's your dime.

He hands her a coin.

INT. CAR—MOVING SHOT
Reuben is driving. No emotion is visible on Norma's face. She stares directly ahead of her. Reuben looks at her once or twice. They are silent. He speaks at last, gently.

REUBEN
The first time you're in is bad.

The planes of her face begin to break up. She fights against it, succeeds for a moment, then gives way. She begins to weep, bitter tears—she has been outraged and demeaned. Tears come hard to her and only an experience like this could bring them.

Reuben gives her time to release it all before he speaks.

REUBEN

It comes with the job. I've seen a pregnant woman on a picket line hit in the stomach with a club. I've seen a boy of sixteen shot in the back. I've seen a man blown to hell and gone when he started his car one morning.
(quietly)
You just got your feet wet on this one.

She stops crying instantly.

INT. HOUSE
Sonny gets up hurriedly as he hears them coming, concern on his face. Norma enters with Reuben behind her. Husband and wife are face-to-face.

SONNY

You all right, Norma?

She nods.

SONNY

I put the kids to bed.

She nods again, then goes past him into the other room.

INT. BEDROOM
In the darkened room, Norma goes to a shelf in the closet and hauls down a metal box. Then she goes from cot to cot and gently wakes the three children, all asleep in the same room.

NORMA

Craig, honey, wake up . . . Millie, honey, it's Momma, get up . . . Alice, sweetheart, come in the other room.

The children get up slowly, rubbing their eyes. She helps them out of bed, shepherds them with her back into the other room.

INT. LIVING ROOM
Norma sits with her children on either side of her, leaning against her, still half-asleep. Alice sprawled in her lap. The two men sit across the room and watch, not intruding.

NORMA

I love you children, that's first. And Sonny loves you. You got both of us. The second thing is, I'm a jailbird. You're gonna hear that and a lot of other things, but you're gonna hear 'em from me first.

The children look up at her, awake now, alert.

NORMA
Millie, your real daddy was named Buddy Wilson and he died four months after you were born. Craig, I never was married to your daddy, and your daddy was not Sonny and not Buddy, but another man. There were some others in my life and they'll be telling you about them too.
(reaches into the box, takes out papers and photographs)
I got pictures of Craig's father in here for him, and pictures of Millie's father for her. Craig, I got settlement papers in here made between me and your daddy; this is your stuff. It's not mine, it's yours. It's your life.
(puts the papers in his lap)
If you go into the mill, I want life to be better for you than it is for me; that's why I joined up with the union and got fired for it.
(pauses)
Now you kids know that I've cleaned out my closet. You know what I am and you know that I believe in standing up for my rights.

She hugs them, each in turn, and they hug her back.

NORMA
Go to the bathroom before you go back to bed.

The children turn and go out of the room, holding their pictures and their papers carefully, as if they were things of value.

ANOTHER ANGLE
Norma rises.

NORMA
I'm gonna go take a bath now. They had lice in that jail.

She walks out of the room, leaving the two men alone. Sonny looks across the room at Reuben trying to assay what position he has in Norma's life.

SONNY
She had one call and she called you.

REUBEN
(shrugs)
She knew I could make bail.

SONNY
You come in here, you mix her up, you turn her head all around. She's all changed. I didn't want her to be a front-runner—I didn't want that. What's gonna happen to us now?

REUBEN
She stood up on a table. She's a free woman. Maybe you can live with it—maybe you can't.

He turns and walks out of the house.

INT. BEDROOM
Norma is in bed, her hands behind her head, awake, silent, turned inward. Sonny enters from the bathroom, ready for bed. His shoes are in his way; he bends to pick them up and move them.

SONNY
Got a broken shoelace . . .

NORMA
There's another pair in the drawer.

SONNY
Busted those last week.

He gets into bed with her. They lie side by side. There is something on his mind, hard to bring forth, hard to articulate. He finally does so, slowly.

SONNY
Did you ever sleep with him?

NORMA
No.
(pauses)
But he's in my head.

Sonny is silent for a long moment.

SONNY
I'll see you through getting tired, getting sick, getting old. I'll see you through anything that comes up. 'Cause there's nobody else in my head. Just you.

He turns out the light, turns his back on her. She lies in the darkened room a moment, then places her hand on his back in a gesture of response.

INT. MILL
The place is jammed, men sweating in the close confines of the room. There are a dozen men with tags across their shirt fronts. A dozen newspaper and television reporters observe and record, flashbulbs going off now and then.

AT THE LONG TABLE
The men here are divided into two groups, half of them BOSSMEN from the company, the other half UNION MEN. Huge stacks of paper ballots are being tabulated from the "NO" and "YES" piles.

The tension is palpable, each piece of paper a victory or a loss. Management is frozen faced and silent. There are no smiles, no talk. Men stand up on chairs to crane and watch the count.

ANOTHER ANGLE
James Brown hoists Bonnie up on his chair, shares it with her so that she too can see. They share hope as the ballots are shuffled, as the two piles diminish, as the silent marks are made, for and against.

IN THE REAR
An OLD MAN, pressed against the wall by the crowd, begins to weep, unable any longer to withstand the suspense. Ashamed, he reaches for a soiled handkerchief, surreptitiously wipes his eyes.

A YOUNG WOMAN
blonde, frail, in the stifling heat and the crush, she suddenly faints.

The pack is so great that she does not fall, is held up by the bodies around her, merely sags against a man beside her. He holds her, takes a knotted kerchief from his neck and mops her brow, looks for a way to get her out. But there is no way, so he supports her in his arms.

FULL SHOT
There is a stir, a final shuffling of feet, then absolute silence as a labor board AGENT raises his hand at the table.

> #### AGENT
> Ballots tabulated for the O.P. Henley Company against the union—three hundred and seventy-three.
> *(pauses, looks at another slip in his hand)*
> Ballots tabulated for the union—four hundred twenty-seven.

EXT. MILL
Norma and Reuben wait outside the gate, hoping to see a figure, to hear a sound, to receive word. This is the moment of promise, the moment of fulfillment.

INT. MILL
There is a tumultuous, roaring shout from the assembled mill hands, a hosanna of triumph. The open-throated outcry goes on and on and on.

EXT. MILL
as Norma and Reuben hear the repeated shouts of "UN-ION, UN-ION, UN-ION."

MOVING SHOT—NORMA AND REUBEN
They step away from the gate, alone, and walk toward the car parked at the curb. Its front seat is sagging under books; suitcases and cartons are jammed in the back, obscuring the rear window.

> NORMA
> You gonna drive straight through?

> REUBEN
> Yeah.

> NORMA
> Better stop for coffee. Stay awake.

> REUBEN
> I got a thermos in the car.

> NORMA
> Well.

> REUBEN
> Well.

They have reached the car.

NORMA AND REUBEN

> REUBEN
> What are you going to do with yourself?

> NORMA
> Live. What else?

REUBEN

Drop me a line once in a while.

NORMA

Does anybody read your mail?

REUBEN

Just my mother.

There is a pause.

REUBEN

I'll send you a copy of Dylan Thomas.

NORMA

I already bought one for myself.

REUBEN

Nobody can do anything for you, huh?

NORMA

You've done something for me. Lots.

REUBEN

You did something for us. A mitzvah.

NORMA

What's that?

REUBEN

A good work.
(pauses)
I never say good-bye. I've been known to cry.

NORMA

What do you say, then?

REUBEN

Be well. Be happy.

NORMA

You, too.

REUBEN

Under the circumstances, best wishes hardly seem enough.
Thanks are in order. Thank you for your companionship,
for your stamina, your horse sense, and a hundred and one

laughs. I also enjoyed looking at your shining hair and shining face.

NORMA

Reuben, I think you like me.

REUBEN

I do.

NORMA

I was gonna get you a tie clip or some shaving lotion, but I didn't know what you'd like.

REUBEN

Norma, what I've had from you has been sumptuous.

He holds out his hand, she holds out hers, they shake. It is no mere ritual of farewell; the touch is held and held and held and held.

But it must end. They are comrades-in-arms, they are battle-weary, they are triumphant. Whatever else they might be remains unspoken.

ANOTHER ANGLE
as Reuben gets into his car and drives away. Norma stands there. She is all there.

FADE OUT

THE END

Irving Ravetch and Harriet Frank, Jr.

1958 *The Long, Hot Summer*
     directed by Martin Ritt
1959 *The Sound and the Fury*
     directed by Martin Ritt
1960 *The Dark at the Top of the Stairs*
     directed by Delbert Mann
1960 *Home from the Hill*
     directed by Vincente Minnelli
1963 *Hud*
     directed by Martin Ritt
1967 *Hombre*
     directed by Martin Ritt
1970 *The Reivers*
     directed by Mark Rydell
1972 *The Cowboys*
     directed by Mark Rydell
1974 *Conrack*
     directed by Martin Ritt
1979 *Norma Rae*
     directed by Martin Ritt
1985 *Murphy's Romance*
     directed by Martin Ritt